HISTORICITY OF LORD JAGANNATHA

CENTRE FOR HUMANIST STUDIES

HISTORICITY OF LORD JAGANNATHA

Sushil Mukherjea

MINERVA : INDIA

MINERVA ASSOCIATES (PUBLICATIONS) PVT. LTD.
7-B, Lake Place : Calcutta-700 029: INDIA

Sponsors: Centre for Humanist Studies, Calcutta -29

(c) Sm. Purna Mukherjee, 1989
First Published: April 1989

1SBN : 81-85195-17-X

Computerised composing :
Laser Printer, 10/2, Ramanath Majumder Street,
Calcutta - 700 009

Printed by :
Pressagents P. Ltd.
2, Bidhan Sarani, Calcutta - 700 006

Published by :
T.K. Mukherjee on behalf of Minerva Associates (Publications)
Pvt. Ltd. 7-B, Lake Place, Calcutta - 700 029

In memory of :-

Nirmal Chandra Gangopadhyay
Dr Hare Krushna Mahtab
Dr V.R. Narla

PREFACE

THIS WORK is a socio-historical analysis of the origin and development of Lord Jagannatha of Puri—how a tribal wooden idol was transformed, in course of time, into a foremost Hindu god. Many well-known scholars have written volumes on Jagannatha. This work should be treated as an additional exploration

In preparing this work the author had to stumble at each step, because of non-availability of early historical materials. Except for some stray findings from archaeological excavations, very little data are available on historic events in Orissa upto the 3rd century A.D. (except for some inscriptions of Asoka and Kharavela). What were available were several myths and legends. It is a sad reflection on Indian culture that our fore-fathers were palpably indifferent towards recording public events of the country. History is no catalogue of dates only, neither is it just a record of certain events related to kings and princes, like wars, conquests, etc. History should be a running and continuous records of facts and events that concern a country and its people; it should enlighten us about our antecedents, tell us how the common people lived, what their social and economic conditions were like, and what role the people had in the matter of governance etc. To quote Toynbee "history can only be of civilizations and not of states". We have been taught instead for generations that *Sruti* (hearsay) and *Smriti* (inner recollection) were God's revelations and therefore these were histories. The *Vedas* were supposed to be not composed by human beings— these were to us God's own words (*Apuruseya*). Similarly, we have been tutored to know the *Ramayana*, the *Mahabharata* and the *Puranas* as histories, though the authors of the first two volumes called their works poetries. In the concluding chapter of the *Ramayana* it is stated that, "This is the first model epic composed by Valmiki" (*Adikavyamidam charsam pura Valmikim Kritam*). In the Adi parva of *Mahabharata* it is found that Lord Brahma said to the author that, "you call your composition as 'kavya' (poetry), so be it known as *kavya*...You should send for Ganesha to take help in preparing the manuscript of the *kavya*". Still, we unhesitatingly term these as histories.

What we call *itihasa* or history is nothing but myths, legends and discourses on *Dharma*, *Artha*, *Kama* and *Moksha*. In his Sanskrit-English dictionary Professor V.S. Apte quotes an ancient *sloka* (verse), which defines what *itihasa* meant to our fore-fathers :

"Dharmarthakamamokshanam   upadeshamamitam   Purbabrityan kathayuktam itihasa prachakshate."

[The past related in the form of a story with the discourses on Dharma (religion), Artha (attainment of riches), Kama (sensual enjoyments) and moksha (deliverance of the soul from recurring births) is called Itihasa]. And hence, study of man and its environs, of man as a socio-politico-economic being, has been totally ignored in our books of history. That kind of uninformed conservatism is still operative even in this age of technological revolution among many of the so-called historians of this country. Except for a handful few, most of their works can at best be called 'cosmetic history'. These are motivated by their mental orientation which is shaped by their bias in religious or political thinking.

Belief in the truth of the religious stories and myths has been systematically ingrained in the mind through a fond attachment to and regular study of the religious scriptures. But such beliefs are nothing but substitutes for ignorance. If one goes through the scriptures, so revered by the Indians, with an open mind, and interpret them rationally, it would be clear how hollow the claim is of the religionists that these were divine ordinations. After all, books are written by human beings, and, therefore, these are not infallible. Whereas religion should have been personalized, in India it has become the single biggest factor that distorts human relations in both public and private life, so much so that it has become the breeding ground of sectarianism and communalism. The present state of affairs in the country bears ample evidence of this unhappy development.

In preparing this work, all available history has been consulted for information about the ruling dynasties, their antecedents, their religious affiliations, and their role in governance. Emphasis has been given on the unearthing of the inner meanings of the relevant myths and legends, particularly those which are current and popular. Attempt has been made to justify the conclusions arrived at rationally and without any bias for any particular religious denomination. Importance has been given to the Savaras, the aborigines, who are the *dayitas* (the beloved) of the Lord. It was felt that without any discussion about the Savaras, their antecedents and religious beliefs, no discussion about the origin and development of the god would be adequate. The roles of religion and politics have also been discussed, insofar as these were responsible for misinterpretating things and confusing the public mind.

If there be any credit for this work, it goes entirely to Bengali culture, one of the sprouts of which is *adda* (informal get-together). Bengalis are very much addicted to such *addas*. It is in such *addas* that they discuss so many things in the earth wherefrom new and novel ideas crop in. It is during one such informal get-together attended by the present author and several friends at a Puri hotel a couple of years back, discussion veered to the peculiar and unconventional image of Jagannatha. The author of this work gave an unorthodox twist to the discussion, which was appreciated by the other friends. One of them, Nirmal Chandra Gangopadhyay, author of several historical and travel books, suggested that when new ideas have come to the surface, the present author should write a book justifying his ideas. In fact, it was he and two other friends, Jyotish Ganguly and Kalidas Banerjee, who, when back in Calcutta, started putting pressure on the author for starting the project of writing the book. Sadly, when the first article titled "Enigma of Lord Jagannatha" was published later in the year in the festival issue of *Bharat Prativa*, a monthly English journal, Nirmal Chandra Gangopadhyay was no more. (Incidentally, the said article has been incorporated in the book *Popular Festivals of India*).

An article on the subject was published in the Puja issue of the Bengali journal *Sanskriti Parikrama* the same year, which attracted the attention of the leading litterateur, Shri Annadasankar Roy, and of the late revered teacher, Professor Nirmal Chandra Bhattacharya. Both of them encouraged the author to write a book on the subject. The author's another article titled "The Mythical Lord Jagannatha" has been incorporated in the book *Life and Culture in Orissa*. The article got good reviews in the Calcutta English dailies. Being commissioned by the Bengali daily *Aaj-Kal* during Rathayatra festival of 1982, the author's article "Jagannath Murtir Rahasya" (Riddle about the image of Jagannatha) was published in three serials on 23rd, 24th and 25th June, 1982, which evoked good response from the readers.

A good number of friends offered their cooperation and guidance. Mention should be made, in particular, of Shri O.K Ghosh, author and scholar, Shri Mihir Sinha, author, Dr Niranjan Dhar, author of several distinguished works on history, Professor Prasanta Kumar Ghosh, at present Principal of Maulana Azad College, Calcutta, Dr Jiten Neogi, medical practitioner and family friend, Shri S.K. Mitra, retired Inspector General of Police, West Bengal, and Shri P.T. Nair, author of several books on history of old Calcutta and some books on Anthropology. All of them went through the first draft and offered substantial assistance. Shri Ghosh took much trouble, advising the author in many ways. Shri Nair got interested in the work and supplied the author with some materials, photographs, etc, without even being asked for these. The author is indebted to them all. Another friend, an artist of repute, Shri Jagadish Banerjee, offered his voluntary service for drawing the cover design of the book. Sincere thanks to him.

Another friend and well-wisher was V.R. Narla, a much known rationalist, former M.P. and leading journalist in the country, editing reputed and established Telugu dailies. Knowing the details of the project, he animated the author from the stupor he was in at that time, and started sending newspaper clippings relating to the subject. Alas, he also passed away sometime back. How happy he would have been to see the book in print.

Neither a historian, nor a social scientist, nor a specialist in any discipline, the author was at first hesitant to publish this work. It was Dr Hare Krushna Mahtab, the noted politician and litterateur, author of a source book on Orissa's history in English and in Oriya, who personally went through the author's Bengali manuscript on the subject, commended the author with the advice of writing an English version of it. He is also no more with us.

Last but not the least, the author is grateful to his wife, members of his family, his mother and his brothers, who, disregarding their beliefs and hardships, offered their unflinching support, particularly in the period when the author had been lying in sick-bed for the last several years. The names of many other friends, who had acted as sources of information and inspiration, could not be given here. The author remembers them all in gratitude.

In conclusion, this must be emphasized that the responsibility for the final shape of the book is with the author and the author alone.

7-B, Lake Place : Calcutta - 700 029
Date: 26 January 1989

CONTENTS

CHAPTER I

INTRODUCTION

LORD JAGANNATHA of Puri has become the subject of a fascinating study, wherein myths, legends, history and religion have got inextricably mixed up. It symbolises a highly eclectic spirit of synthesis– an amalgam of effects of imposed cults and cultures. Here primitive cults merge with different Indian and Hindu religious denominations like Jainism, Buddhism, Tantricism, Saivism, Vaishnavism, etc. Hence, it can be said that Jagannatha is not just a deity, it is a unique institution.

The incongruous, malformed look of Jagannatha (Lord of the Universe) is most unconventional and as such it draws instant attention. There are numerous deities in the Hindu pantheon of gods and goddesses, and their images, however ferocious and cruel the deity may be, are artistically carved– images essentially of men and women, delineated with majesty and profundity. But the Lord Jagannatha is not designed in the likeness of a human being– a massive square head and chest merge into one piece of wooden stump without any demarcation for the neck; arms have been separately inserted in a line with the upper lip; it has very large and bizzare looking eyes; and the waist is the limit of the body. In short, it looks odious. Apart from the image itself, there are other inconsistencies that come to everybody's notice. Possibly this is the only Hindu temple in India where two brothers and their sister in between them are placed on the same *bedi* (platform) for the *pujas*. Rituals concerning the *pujas* in the temple are also at variance with known Hindu rituals. Moreover, in this Puri temple of Jagannatha many major functions are performed not only by the Brahmin priests, but also by the aboriginals caled Savaras (Saora in common parlance), which goes against all normal canons of Hindu ritualism. Additionally, whereas the Hindu gods and goddesses are modelled in stone or clay, this image is made from the wood of the *neem* tree (*Melia azadiracta*).

Many legends have been woven around this god. These legends are in actuality attempts to convince people of its being a Jaina deity/ Buddhist deity/ Shaiva-Shakta deity/and/or Vaishnava deity. It has also been noticed that all kings of Orissa since early times have respected and worshipped this deity with pomp and due reverence, irrespective of their beliefs in different Indian/Hindu religious persuasions. Volumes have been written on this Lord of the Universe, in which the authors were guided by a motivation to establish the connection of this deity with their own brand of religious 'isms'.

This queer form of the image of the Lord naturally evokes intense interest. The questions that come up in the mind are — why is there such a rude image? Which gods and goddesses do this trinity represent? Why is the Lord painted black, when Balabhadra is painted white, and Subhadra golden? Does this indicate that the Lord symbolises Shri Krishna? And why do the aborigines occupy an exalted position in the temple activities? Many such questions throng the minds of the visitors, even of the believers themselves.

Before assessing and asseverating anything, it is felt that the past socio-political history of Orissa should be discussed, since it may help in untying knots and giving us a clear picture of the background. This should also include the past history and religious beliefs of the Savaras, who are termed as *dayitas* (near and dear ones) of the Lord, as well as a consideration of the rise and decline of different religious movements in Orissa.

Socio-Political Background

Orissa has not only made a vital contribution to the religious culture centring around Lord Jagannatha, its ancient political history was also glorious. The inhabitants of this region were reckoned as a martial race, and they are mentioned as such in the *Mahabharata* and the *Puranas*. Present day Orissa comprises parts of ancient Utkala, Odradesha, Kosala and Kalinga. The nomenclature of this state as Orissa is a new one. Let us discuss in capsule the history and topography of these four regions, which now make up the territory of Orissa.

Utkala

The ancient name is Ukkhala. Utkala has been mentioned in the *Mahabharata*, which establishes its antiquity. In the early Puranas like *Matsya, Vayu,* etc. and also in Kalidasa's *Raghuvamsam* the Utkala kingdom signifies an area near the Vindhya mountains. Pargiter in his *The Purana Text of the Dynasties of Kali Age* records Utkala to be in the south of Chhotanagpur. In the middle ages Utkala was described as the area from the Midnapore district (now in West Bengal) to the coastal area of the Puri district. Utkala has also been mentioned in the ancient Buddhist scriptures *Mahabhaggas* and the *Jatakas*. In the Bhishmaparva of the *Mahabharata* the inhabitants of Utkala have been denigrated with harsh words, and they have been termed as wild and rude. The *Markandeya Purana* described the natives of this area as cruel and barbaric, inhabiting the area since ancient days, and remarked that they were so conceited that they wanted to remain aloof from others, and did not even maintain contacts with the people of the neighbouring areas. Utkala joined the forces of the Pandavas in the Mahabharata War. The name of the region as Utkala derives from the Utkala or Ukkhala tribe, which had been dominating in this area. During the rule of the Nandas and Mauryas, and even during the time of King Kharavela, Utkala had no political importance. At that time this area was known as Toshali. The name Utkala revived for some time from the 4th century A.D. From the *Raghuvamsam* of Kalidasa (5th century) it is known that Utkala was a neighbouring state of Kalinga, and its area was in between Kapila river (present day Kasai) of Midnapore district and the northern boundary of Kalinga. Again, it went downhill for a long period, and it was only in the 11th century, during the Soma dynasty's rule, that Utkala could raise its head again with its pristine glory.

From the Soro copper plates (580 A.D) in the district of Balasore we come to know that at that time Utkala area was known as North Toshali. In the 7th century King Somadatta, a vassal king of Maharaja Sasanka of Karnasuvarna, renamed North Toshali as Utkala. After the death of Sasanka, Harsavardhana conquered Utkala and other neighbouring states, and named the area as Odravisaya. In the middle of the 11th century, the entire area, comprising of North and South Toshali, Kalinga, and Kosala, came under one kingdom controlled by the Soma dynasty and was designated as Utkala, with its capital at Yayatinagara in the district of Phulbani. This Yayatinagara was built in the 10th century by Yayati Mahasivagupta the First. From the Soro copper plates it is known that the earliest capital of Utkala was at Viraja, i.e. Jajpur. After the fall of the Soma dynasty, the Ganga dynasty came to power and they established a new capital town of Utkala at Cuttack and named it as Abhinava Varanasi. After the end of the Ganga rule the power vested with the Surya dynastic kings, who changed the name of their kingdom from Utkala to Odisa. The name Utkala then became erased.

After the British occupation of the country this state became known as Orissa.

Odradesa

Odisa is the Oriya synonym of Odradesa. The name signifies that the area was inhabited by the aboriginal people known as Odras/ Udras. Numerically this Odra tribe is almost extinct; they have mostly merged with the Hindu mainstream. A few who still prefer to call themselves Odras are tilling land at Dhenkanal and near about places. As this area was known after them, it can be assumed that in ancient days they were a powerful tribe. Odras have also been mentioned in the *Mahabharata.* Along with other tribal groups they have been mentioned in the *Manusamhita.* From the Soro copper plates it is known that this area was then a part of North Toshali. In his *Natyashastra* (6th century A.D.) Bharat Muni has remarked that in this area Odras were living along with the Savaras and other wild tribes. Pliny (1st century A.D.) in his *Natural History* listed Indian tribes, where he has mentioned that in the Meleus mountain region two tribes "Maledes" and "Suaries" live. Meleus is today's Malyaban mountain in Dhenkanal, and Maledes and Suaries are Munda and Savara tribes. Hieun Tsang mentions Odra as a kingdom. During the first part of the 11th century the famous Muslim historian Al-Beruni called this area as "Udrabhisa". In the later part of the 14th century another Muslim historian, Shams-al Din-Siraj records this area as "Jajpur-Odisa". In the Tirumalai inscription of 1025 A.D.it has been recorded that Odrabisaya is the neighbouring state of Kosala. The Dirghangi inscription of 1075 A.D. mentions that Utkala and Odra were contiguous states. In the various inscriptions left by the Soma dynastic kings Odradesa has been specified as lying between Kosala and Utkala. Poet Sarala Dasa of the Oriya *Mahabharata* fame termed this area as "Oda State" or "Odisa". The well-known scholar, General Cunningham, while describing the boundary of this state in his book *The Ancient Geography of India,* has remarked that this ancient state spread out in the Mahanadi delta and the lower part of the river Suvarnarekha. He has stated that present day Cuttack and some parts of the present Sambalpur district were within this state. From Chhatisgarh and Sambalpur epigraphic records one gathers that the mountainous region in between Kalinga and South Kosala, i.e. from the southern mountainous region of Keonjhar and Mayurbhanj to the Mahanadi coastal area, was called Odrabhumi. The Tibetan historian Lama Taranath refers to Orissa as Odibhisa.

So, it can be safely assumed that like Utkala, the kingdom of Odradesa was also of antiquity.

Kalinga

The existence of Kalinga can also be traced back to remote antiquity. In the *Mahabharata* Kalinga has been specifically mentioned because of its soldiers' indomitable courage in war and of its well-trained elephants. The Kalinga king was Duryodhana's ally, and his courage and martial qualities surprised Duryodhana, who desired that if necessary after Karna the Kalinga king should be declared as the Commander of the Kaurava forces. His team of elephants created terror and panic among the Pandavas. Though the definite boundary of Kalinga has not been stated in the *Mahabharata,* in its Vanaparva the mouth of the Ganges has been mentioned as its northern limit. Megasthenes also concurred in this. Pliny divided Kalinga into three parts— Gangaridas Kalinga, Macco-Kalinga, and Kalinga. It can be assumed that at that early period Kalinga's expanse was between the mouth of the Ganges and that of the Godavari. In the *Matsya Purana*, Amarkantaka mountain in the present day Madhya Pradesh has been described as the Western boundary of Kalinga.

During the 4th century B.C Mahapadma Nanda occupied the coastal area of Kalinga and brought this area under the domination of Magadha. It was he who took along with him the "Kalinga Jeena" image, treating it as a symbol of occupation of Kalinga. From the name of the image it can be assumed that it was that of some Jaina Tirthankara. R.D. Banerjee in his book *History of Orissa* has described it as the image of the tenth Tirthankara Seetalanatha. Another opinion is that it was of the first Tirthankara, Risavadeva. At the time of Chandragupta's ascendancy in Magadha, Kalinga was not only an independent kingdom, it was also recognised as one of the main rival forces against the Mauryas. After defeating the Greek Commander Seleukos, Chandragupta occupied a vast domain from Kabul and Kandahar in the north to the southern part of India, but even then he did not invade Kalinga, which was contiguous to Magadha. Thus, it can safely be presumed that at that time Kalinga was regarded as a mighty kingdom. An idea of Kalinga's might can be ascertained from Megasthenes' accounts. He stated that the massive and well-trained elephant troops of Kalinga were awe-inspiring. He estimated that Kalinga possessed 60 thousand infantry, one thousand cavalry, and 700 trained elephants— a force which was ever straining at the leash for war. Bindusara inherited the throne of Magadha from Chandragupta, and he also did not attempt to invade Kalinga. It was the third Maurya King, Asoka, who invaded Kalinga— Asoka who at that time was known as "Chandasoka" (Asoka the terrible) for his ruthless behaviour. Kalinga was then not only known to possess a mighty land force, but also a strong naval force, and it had extensive mercantile relations with overseas countries.

In the early days of the historic period, i.e. during the 6th century B.C., Kalinga was a well-known kingdom in India. In Jaina and Buddhist literatures much has been said about the kings of Kalinga. After the death of the Lord Buddha, the Buddhist monk Kshema Thera brought one tooth (from the left jaw) of the Buddha as a relic from Kushinagar to Kalinga, and he handed over the relic to the Kalinga king Brahmadatta for its safety and proper maintenance. This incident indicates that at that time Buddhism was a dominant religion there. In the Jaina literature it has been noted that at different periods the kings of Kalinga were influenced by the teachings of Parshwanatha and Mahavira. So, it can safely be said that in the ancient period Kalinga interacted with the Indian religious and cultural mainstream.

Kalinga's geographical position was such that for an easy access to the southern part of the country from the northern side, Kalinga had to be crossed. To avoid wars with Kalinga, earlier kings skirted the Kalinga borders to reach the southern part of the country. Apart from its location in between the south and the north of the country, Kalinga's dominance along the eastern coast from the estuary of the Ganges was an obstacle to Magadha's navigational outlet. And so, Asoka became determined to invade and occupy Kalinga. He did so in 261 B.C. It can be well assumed that at the time of invasion Asoka brought up with him a colossal force. From Asokan edicts it is known that in the war with Kalinga 1,00,000 soldiers died, 1,50,000 became captive, and the total number of deaths was much more. From this we can understand that both the sides mustered huge forces. The terrible and heart-rending consequences of this war changed Asoka from "Chandasoka" to "Dharmasoka" (Asoka the Pious) ; since then he avoided wars and became a religious person. Under Asoka the capital of Kalinga was Toshali. It has now been ascertained that the present Dhauli village in the district of Puri was the Toshali of Asoka. The Asokan edicts on the Dhauli mountain point to this.

Kalinga came to the forefront of Indian history again in the Ist century B.C during the reign of the King Kharavela. He belonged to the Cheta dynasty of Magadha, but its rulers mamed themselves as of the Mahameghavahana dynasty. Kharavela was the third in that line. He became known as a mighty emperor, as under him Kalinga became a kingdom of vast extent. Quite a big part of the Deccan became subordinate to Kalinga. It is said that he even defeated the mighty Satavahana emperor Satakarni (on this point there remains a controversy among the historians). In the South, the Chola, Pandya, Satyaputra, Keralaputra and Tamraparni kings had allied themselves under treaties for their own interests, and this alliance remained in vogue for a long time. This allied force could maintain its independence even during Mauryan rule. But in the war with Kharavela they got defeated. When the city of Mathura in the northern part of the country was being devastated by the Indo-Greek Yavana king Demetrius, emperor Kharavela marched to that city and saved it from "Dimita". He also occupied Magadha and brought back therefrom the "Kalinga Jeena" image that had been plundered by Mahapadma Nanda centuries back.

Kalinganagari was chosen to be the capital city by Kharavela. Sishupalgarh near Bhubaneswar has been determined to be this Kalinganagari. Kharavela was a devotee of Jainism. At the last lap of his life, after recovering the "Kalinga Jeena", he devoted himself to religious work. There is no doubt that during the reign of Kharavela, Kalinga was in a supreme position in the field of education, sculpture and administration. The well-known Hatigumpha inscriptions in the caves of Khandagiri at Bhubaneswar are those of Kharavela. From these inscriptions it is known that he took great interest in aesthetics, mathematics, social laws, and legal matters. It is also known that Pithunda was the capital city of ancient Kalinga. It seems that the Greek historian Ptolemy called Pithunda as Pitundra. In the early Jaina literature Pithuda-Pihunda city was described as the most important place of the Jainas. It is presumed that Mahapadma Nanda had plundered this old city, taking away the "Kalinga Jeena" from there. The location of this city was somewhere on the sea coast between the Godavari and Mahanadi rivers. Another source says that the early capital city of Kalinga was Singhapura, present day Singupuram in the district of Sri Kakulam. In the

4th century A.D. during the rule of the Matharas, Kalinga's capital was transferred to Singhapura.

It is inferred that Jainism obtained its foothold in Kalinga before the 5th century B.C. These sources say that the Jaina gurus Parshwanatha, Mahavira and others toured Kalinga. Possibly, among the non-Hindu religious orders, besides existing primitive beliefs in Shaktism, etc., Jainism was the first such order to capture the minds of the Kalingans. It is to be noted that though Kharavela was a devout Jaina, he was liberal enough to tolerate different religious ideas and practices. Kharavela also did much for the economic and social development of Kalinga. After his death, however, a black curtain comes down. Practically nothing is known about this dynasty's decline.

Kalinga comes to prominence again during the later part of the 3rd century A.D. The southern part of Kalinga was then under the domination of the Matharas, who were initially followers of Jainism. Hieun Tsang observed that in the year 639 A.D. when he was travelling through Orissa, the country was then divided into three parts -- Odra, Kalinga, and Kongoda. He remarked that there were only 50 Hindu temples in Odra, 100 in Kongoda, whereas the number of tirthikas (Jaina monasteries) were more than ten thousand. He also said that in spite of functioning of various religious groups in Kalinga, the followers of Jainism were in considerable majority.

At the time of the Gupta emperor Samudra Gupta's invasion of Kalinga, it was divided into many small kingdoms. While marching through Kalinga towards the Deccan, Samudra Gupta had to fight with a few independent kings of Orissa, important among whom were Mahendra of Kosala, Vyaghraraja of Mahakantara, Mantaraja of Kurala, Mahendragiri of Pistapura, Swamidatta of Kettua, Damana of Erandapalli, and Kuvera of Devarastra. After Samudra Gupta's invasion of Kalinga, we find two dynasties, who established independent kingdoms at the south of the Mahendra mountain -- Pitribhaktas and Matharas (364-540 A.D.).

At the later part of the 4th century, during the rule of the Matharas, Kalinga could revive a part of its old glory, but could not get back the old territory. At that time Kalinga's boundary was in between the Godavari river and the Mahanadi. The Matharas, of course, proclaimed themselves as Kalingadhipati (Master of Kalinga). During the 150 years rule of the Matharas,

Brahminism could raise its head in the religious and cultural domain of Kalinga. The learning of Sanskrit was patronised by the Matharas. During that period Kalinga could extend its external trade through the seas

In the 5th and 6th centuries the Sailodbhava dynasty had been ruling in the southern coastal area of Kalinga. This area was then known as Kongoda. It is presumed that this aboriginal dynasty was earlier in control of the mountainous area around the Chilika lakes and Ganjam. It is also said that this dynasty occupied Suvarnadwipa in the South East Asia, and established the Sailendra kingdom there. During the second half of the 6th century we come to know of another dynasty, belonging to the aboriginal group, known as the Nala dynasty. They had been ruling over the districts of Koraput and Kalahandi of Orissa and over the Bastar area of Madhya Pradesh.

After the decline of the Matharas some parts of Kalinga, from the Rishikulya river on the north to Nagaveli of Ganjam district in the south, came under the domination of the Ganga dynasty. This dynasty has ancientness. Megasthenes called it as Gangaridai and observed that the area in which the Gangaridas lived was bounded by the Ganges in the north, river Damodara in the south, the sea in the east, and Magadha in the west. From the area described by Megasthenes it can be ascertained that the early home of the Ganga dynasty was in West Bengal. Though no classical Indian account mentions Gangaridai as a mighty kingdom, Didorus wrote, "India....is inhabited by very many nations among which the greatest of all is that of Gangaridas, against whom Alexander did not undertake an expedition, being deterred by the multitude of their elephants." (P.S. Banerjee in *Illustrated Weekly of India*, 12.5.85). According to Pliny this dynasty started travelling south, and the group which settled in Orissa were known as the Eastern Gangas. Another group went further south and established their domain in the southern part of Mysore. In the 5th century they were ruling over a part of Kalinga, then known as Trikalinga (in between the rivers Jhanjhavati and Vedavati). They stayed put in this area for about 600 years. It was during the 11th century that they became powerful enough to bring in other parts of Kalinga under their wings.

In the political history of Orissa, after the Matharas and Sailodbhava dynasties, we come to know of another dynasty, known as Bhauma-Karas. Their contribution towards the evolution of present day Orissa was significant. One ruler of this dynasty, Subhakaradeva the First, wrote a religious book and sent it as his gift to the then Chinese emperor Te-tsung (*Epigraphica India*). During this time, i.e. during the later part of the 8th century, a university was established at Puspagiri in Orissa. This university became so famous that the Chinese traveller Hiuen Tsang mentioned it in his travel diary. During the later part of the Bhauma-Kara rule, we come to know of another dynasty known as the Soma, who were ruling over the Kosala part of Orissa. The Bhauma-Karas at that time were reigning over the Utkala part. The Bhauma-Karas were Buddhists, but they also bore a liberal attitude towards other religions. While the Bhauma-Karas were at the declining stage, the Shaivites started gaining ground in Orissa. These Bhauma-Karas are also supposed to be of the aboriginal tribe, Bhumija by name.

The social and cultural development that started in Orissa during the Bhauma-Kara rule continued during the rule of the Somas. The Soma king Yayati Mahashivagupta the First took the title "Kesari", and he could bring Utkala and Kosala under his kingdom. Yayati the First took active interest in building temples, and during his time Bhubaneswar became known as the city of temples. It is said that Yayati the First performed more than one *Aswamedha Yajna* (horse sacrifice rite) at Jajpur and on these occasions he invited ten thousand Brahmins to Kalinga from Kanauj. It will thus not be wrong to remark that it was Yayati the First who can be designated as the real initiator of Brahminism in Orissa. Yayati the Second of this dynasty was also a mighty king. He brought under his rule all the then four divisions of Orissa, and proclaimed himself as the Emperor of Kalinga-Utkala-Kongoda-Kosala. It was during the reign of Janamejaya II, son of Udyota Kesari, that decline and disintegration of this dynasty started. This situation brought in opportunities for the Gangas, who had been waiting in the wings since long, and who ultimately replaced the Kesaris on the throne of Orissa. During their reign the capital was transferred to Mukhalingam on the coast of the Vansadhara river near Parlakemadi. The Ganga King Anantavarman Choraganga claimed Kalinga to be the mightiest Hindu kingdom at that time in the country. During his time Kalinga spread out between the Ganges and Godavari. His father was a Ganga, but his mother belonged to the Chola dynasty of the south, for which he termed himself as Cholaganga or Choraganga. In the year 1135 he transferred his capital from Mukhalingam (then known as Kalinganagar) to Cuttack, and he named his empire as " Sakalotkala " (entire

Utkala). The Jagannatha temple, as we see it today, was planned by him, and he started its construction work also. In the last period of his life he devoted himself to religious work and took the principal role in establishing Vaishnavism in Orissa.

From Anantavarman onwards fifteen kings of this family could maintain control of this kingdom. Another important king of this dynasty was Narasinhadeva the First, who was known for his valour and might. He defeated the Sultans of Bengal twice, and occupied Lakshmanavati, the then capital of Bengal, in the years 1243 and 1244. After the death of Anantavarman this Hindu kingdom had to face several sporadic attempts by the Muslim forces from the neighbouring areas. Narasinhadeva not only defeated them in the wars, he could also occupy several districts from the Sultanate of Bengal and he incorporated the area in his kingdom. He was thus able to maintain his border at the river Ganges. It was he who built the world famous temple at Konark, known as the Sun temple. During Ganga rule though Telugu was the language of the kings, Oriya language and literature started developing– there was marked improvement in the Oriya alphabet, Oriya prose and its style. So, during the three hundred years rule by the Gangas in Orissa, they not only expanded the area of their empire, Oriya language and literature prospered, there was a marked stability in the sphere of politics and economics, and Orissa became prominent in the fields of art, literature and religion.

It has been mentioned that Anantavarman Choraganga had taken initiative in giving a good footing to Vaishnavism in Orissa. Earlier these Gangas were Shaivites, and Anantavarman himself was a devotee of Shiva. It is said that during his rule Ramanuja travelled in Orissa and he inspired Anantavarman to Vaishnavism. This Ganga dynasty occupied the southern region of the Mahendra mountain during the later part of the 5th century. At that time they accepted Shiva Gokarnaswami, the god of the Savaras at the Mahendra mountain, to be their own god. In the Visakhapatnam inscription of 1119, Anantavarman Choraganga stated that, "After Kamarnava was annointed with the tilakas (sectarian mark painted on the forehead) meant for a king and with the blessings of the Lord Shiva-Gokarnaswami, he came down from the mountain and occupied Kalinga by killing the king of the Savaras". This Lord Gokarnaswami was being worshipped by the Gangas as their own god till the 12th century. Khila Munda is the aboriginal name of this god.

The end of the Ganga rule can be called an accident. The last Ganga king had no children, and the power of the kingdom went peacefully to the control of Kapilendra Rout Roy. He founded a new dynasty known as Suryabamsha (Solar dynasty). The *Madala Panji* (chronicles kept in the Jagannatha temple) gives a fantastic story about this bloodless transference of power. Besides this there is another rational version. According to this story, the last Ganga King was a weak and inefficient person, and as he had no child, the ministers and aristocrats decided to appoint a new King. They found in Kapilendra Deva a person of indomitable courage, possessing the quality of leadership, and they decided to put him on the throne. At that time Kapilendra was a General in the Kalingan army.

The history of Kalinga should end at this point, as Kapilandra Deva renamed Kalinga as Odisa. And this nomenclature "Odisa" ultimately became Orissa during the British rule.

Kosala

From the *Ramayana* we come to know that after the death of Ramachandra, the kingdom of Kosala was divided in two parts – Lava was entrusted with North Kosala with its capital city at Shravasti, and Kusha with South Kosala in and around the Vindhyas. From Buddhist literature we come to know that during the time of Lord Buddha, North Kosala and South Kosala were two different kingdoms. In the Vanaparva of the *Mahabharata* it has been mentioned that the location of Kosala was in the north of the Deccan. In the different *Puranas* Kosala has been described as the area in and around the Vindhyas. Hiuen Tsang in his travel diary mentioned that the capital of Kosala was near the capital city of Kalinga. It is presumed that Bilaspur and Raipur districts of the present day Madhya Pradesh, and Sundargarh, Bolangir, and Sambalpur districts of present day Orissa, taken together, was the area which was called Kosala, and the capital city of Kosala at that time was Sripura (Sirpur) on the Mahanadi coast in the district of Raipur. The Tirumalai inscription of 1025 mentions Odravisaya and Kosala along with another kingdom, Sakkarkota. From different inscriptions found in Chhatisgarh and Sambalpur area it is found that in ancient times Kosala comprised of the entire Sambalpur district and twenty other vassal states, the mountainous region in between Kalinga and Kosala was Odradesa, and Utkala was in the north of Odradesa.

B.C. Majumdar in his book *Typical Selections from Oriya Literature* has remarked that in the seventh century a group of Hinduized Savaras had been ruling over Kosala and they established their capital at Sirpur in the north of Raipur. King Tivaradeva of this dynasty was a very powerful king in the 8th century. After his death his nephew Balarjuna sat on the throne and took the title Mahashivagupta. One of the queens of this dynasty belonged to the Gupta dynasty of Magadha. Because of such a royal connection Balarjuna has been described as a pure kshatriya. The children of Balarjuna failed to keep control over the kingdom and shifted to a small region outside the districts of Raipur and Bilaspur. After a long period we come across another Mahashivagupta, who became the Maharaja of Kosala and Tri-Kalinga. And this Mahashivagupta is the King Yayati · Kesari the First of the Soma dynasty. Majumdar remarks that this Yayati Kesari belongs to the family of Balarjuna.

During the initial days of the Soma dynasty's rule they faced rivalry from another dynasty, known as Kalachuri, for which they had to continuously shift their capital. Ultimately they established it at Yayatinagara in the district of Phulbani. In the 11th century Yayati the Second brought Utkala under his control. But within a short period he separated Utkala from Kosala, for political reasons, and established two capitals— one at Yayatinagara for Utkala, and the other at Subarnapura at the junction of the Mahanadi and Tel rivers for Kosala. The later part of the 11th century saw the Soma kings defeated by the Cholas, who took over the control of Kosala from them, but soon after the Cholas became dispossessed of the area by the Kalachuris. Ultimately in 1112 the Gangas defeated the Kalachuris and brought the districts of Sambalpur and Bolangir under their control. Till the mid-14th century this area was ruled by the Gangas. At the declining stages of the Ganga rule a new force raised its head in the Kosala area it consisted of the Rajput Chauhans, operating from Patna in Bolangir district, who brought Kosala under their control. It was during the rule of the Surya dynasty that Kosala was again integrated with Orissa.

We have come across the names of Kongoda and Tri-Kalinga, two small kingdoms, during the course of narration about Odradesa, Utkala, Kalinga, and Kosala. A brief narration of these two states is being done here.

Kongoda

When the Sailodbhava dynasty was ruling in southern coastal area of Kalinga, during the 5th-6th centuries, the area was mentioned as Kongoda. This name did not crop up earlier. Scholars surmise that the area in between the Chilika lakes and Ganjam was Kongoda, Kongoda was again mentioned when we find the Soma King Yayati the Second as the ruler of this kingdom. This was integrated with Kalinga, and so we do not hear of it later on as a separate unit.

Tri-Kalinga

From several inscriptions we come to know of the existence of Tri-Kalinga for some time According to *Ancient India* of McCrindle, Tri-Kalinga is the same area which was described by Pliny as Macco-Kalinga. Tri-Kalinga has been mentioned in the Jirjingi copper plate (537 A.D.) of Indravarman the First of the Eastern Ganga dynasty. According to Anantavarman Choraganga, Tri-Kalinga was founded by Kama-rnava Deva, the ancestor of the Eastern Ganga dynasty. Even in the copper plates of the Eastern Chalukyas, Kalinga and Tri-Kalinga have been mentioned. From different inscriptions and literary sources it appears that the boundary limit of Tri-Kalinga was Maharashtra in the west, Kalinga in the east, Pandya in the south, and Kanyakubja in the north.

While discussing the political history of Kalinga we have been traversing through Kosala and other regions of ancient Orissa. We now come back to Odisa state, by which name the Surya King Kapilendra Deva designated Orissa, soon after his coming to power. When in 1436 Kapilendra Deva took over the reign of the kingdom, several neighbouring states, which had then become strong, were planning to subvert Orissa on one side was the Bengal Sultanate, and on the other side, from the south, the Bahmani kingdom and the Vijayanagara empire. Kapilendra Deva took the offensive, and defeating all of them in wars, expanded his kingdom from the western coast of the river Hugli to Kondavidu after crossing the river Krishna in the south, and the major portion of the coastal area of Tamilnadu. So, we find that the total expanse of his kingdom was from the Ganges to the Kaveri river. Thereafter he proclaimed himself as "Gajapati, Gaudeshwara, Navakoti- Karnata- Kalavages- hwara". In fact, after king Kharavela, Kapilendra Deva was the only king of Orissa who could expand the area of this kingdom to such

In extent. Mighty warrior he was, but he was also a cultured person. He wrote a Sanskrit drama titled *Parasurama Vijaya*. It was during his time, it is supposed, that the celebrated poet Sudramani Sarala Dasa composed in Oriya his *Mahabharata*, which is acknowledged as a classic.

After his death in 1466 his son Purushottama Deva inherited the throne. He was a man of enlightenment, and composed several books. He wrote in Sanskrit a volume titled *Nava Malika*, in which he recorded summaries of 67 *Puranas*. His other works were *Abhinava Gitagovinda*, a collection of poems, *Durgotsava, Mukti Chintamani, Visnu-Bhakti Kalpadruma*. M.N. Das "Ancient and Medieval Empries and Kingdoms" in *History and Culture of Orissa*, p.101). During his reign he had also to face attacks from the Vijayanagara empire and the Bahmani kingdom. But he was able to frustrate the aggressors' attempts. Prataparudra Deva was the next king to ascend the throne of Orissa in 1497. Like his father he too was well educated and cultured. He was also known to be a very religious king. During his reign, upto 1540, Orissa lost much of its territory, particularly portions of Bengal and a major part of the south. The area of the present day Orissa was almost what Prataparudra Deva could keep control of. For some time past a plot was being hatched round the throne, and this become effective during the rule of Prataparudra Deva. A section of priests of the Jagannatha temple had been in conspiracy with a section of the ministers against the king. Defeat in the wars and consequent loss of territory opened up an opportunity to the conspirators to thicken the plot against the king. For the purpose of gaining legitimacy the Ganga and Surya Kings had vested the kingdom in the name of Lord Jagannatha. Though the plot against the kings started during Ganga rule, it could become effective only during Prataparudra Deva's time. As the kings of Orissa since the time of the Gangas were trying to give more time to temple affairs, priests of the temple were not at all kind to this gesture of the kings. Prataparudra Deva become a disciple of Sri Chaitanya, which was not at all liked by a section of the priests who had then been feeling cornered by the influence of Sri Chaitanya. The leadership of the plot was taken by Govind Vidyadhara, who was a General in the army (some scholars say that he was a Minister of Prataparudra Deva). After the death of Sri Chaitanya (or murder ?), the conspirators became up-and-coming in their plot. Soon after Prataparudra Deva died, two of his sons were put on the throne one after another, but both of them lost their lives within a short period

at the hands of the conspirators. Govind Vidyadhara thereafte
ascended the throne. He became the symbol of the decline an
end of Orissa's glory. Orissa lost its splendour and independenc
soon after. After the Surya dynasty, it was successively ruled b
the Bhoi Kings, the patriarch of which was Govind Vidyadhara
Afghans, Mughals, Marathas, and ultimately by the Britishers.

APPENDIX

RECORDED HISTORY in our country is of recent vogue. It is a sorry feature of our culture that the Hindus were all along allergic to recording their history, in spite of the fact that they ruled over the country for centuries. It is because of the non-availability of recorded history that confusion abounds. Scholars, who are trying to reconstruct it, are finding it difficult to organise it, as whatever time tables are available differ so much with one another that it becomes difficult to reach any conclusion. The only bright aspect are the archaeological findings. But the progress of such work is so slow for various reasons, that one does not know when scholars will be able to formulate their final findings, from which society will, no doubt, benefit. It is because of the archaeological works that it has been possible to know something about the past. As there is no recorded history, there is no alternative to know of our past or to come near it than through archaeological excavations. The history of Orissa is also no exception to this. We know very little of its hoary past. It was from the Asokan edicts that the time of the Kalinga war could be ascertained. After that period what happened in Orissa is not known. Later on we come to know of the King Kharavela and his activities from the Hatigumpha inscriptions. Nothing is again heard of Orissa after Kharavela. Though there has been found a time table upto the Soma dynasty's rule, these are based, more or less, on assumptions. It is only after that period that we can partly depend on records. The following time-table has been prepared on the basis of studies of eminent scholars like. Dr B.M. Barua, Dr H.K. Mahtab, Dr D.C. Sarkar, Dr N.K. Sahu, Dr K.C. Panigrahi, etc.

261 B.C	-Invasion of Kalinga by Asoka
1st Century B.C.	-Mahameghabahana dynasty
4th-5th Century A.D.-	Matharas dynasty in south Orissa; Vasishtha and Pitribhakta Sri Ramakasyap dynasty in Kosala
5th-7th Century	-Nala dynasty in south Kosala; Stambheshwari Padabhaktas in West Orissa; Bigraha and Moudgalya in north Orissa; Mana dynasty from Balasore to Puri (King Sambhuyasa); and Sailodbhava dynasty in Kongoda
736 - 923 A.D.	-Bhauma-Kara dynasty for entire Orissa; for some time Pandu

	dynasty in south Kosala
882 - 1110 A.D.	-Soma dynasty, initially in the Sonepore area, later entire Orissa. For some time Kalachur dynasty in Sonepore area
1038 - 1434 A.D.	-East Ganga dynasty– from 1110 entire Orissa
1434 - 1542 A.D.	-Surya dynasty
1542 - 1560 A.D	-Bhoi dynasty
1560 - 1568 A.D.	-Last Hindu king Mukunda Deva

CHAPTER II

INDIAN CULTURE AND THE ABORIGINES

THE ABORIGINAL population of India comprises 25% of the total, and about 23% of Orissa's population consists of aboriginal groups. As per 1981 Census 62 tribal groups, numbering 59,15,067 are recognised, and more than 25% of such population live in the districts of Sundargarh, Mayurbhanj, Phulbani, Koraput, Keonjhar, Kalahandi, Sambalpur and Bolangir. They concentrate more thickly in the mountain and forest zones than valleys or towns. In Orissa the backward classes, including the aborigines, consists of about 66.7% of its population. Certain groups in Orissa have till now maintained their distinct existence as aborigines. Among them are Kondhs, Gonds, Hill Saoras (Savars), Bhuiyas, Santhals, and Bhimjal tribes. Dr Harekrushna Mahtab *(History of Orissa)* and Dr Mayadhar Mansinha *(Saga of the Land of Lord Jagannatha)* are of the opinion that those aboriginal tribes in whose names regions were named as "Odradesa" "Kalinga", and "Utkala" failed to maintain, with the passage of time, their own separate existence.

Thousand of years' intermingling and intermixing have brought in many dramatic changes, because of which there are no perceptible dividing line between the Hindus and the aborigines. This line has blurred because of admixture of blood, and such admixture has been going on since the Vedic age. Lord Krishna is regarded as a Hindu deity, but there is a legend that his mother belonged to an aboriginal tribe. It appears from various facts, as will be shown, that Lord Jagannatha himself had been, in the initial stage, a deity of the aboriginal Savaras. A major portion of those who were originally Savaras do not now want to be recognised as aboriginals. Most of them have been converted either to Hinduism or Christianity. Not only in the matter of religion, but also in their social customs and manners they are one with the mainstream. The Savara *dayitapati* (chief of the *dayitas*) gets married into the upper class Hindu families. Those Savaras, who could not join the mainstream, are known as Hill Saoras or wild Savaras, and they live in the forest and mountains.

Interestingly, though different ruling dynasties of Orissa proclaimed themselves as Kshatriyas by taking such pretentious titles as belonging to Lunar (Soma), Solar (Surjya) or other

dynasty, in reality most of them were of aboriginal heredity–
they carry the blood of Kondhs, Gonds, Savaras, Bhuiyas, Sulkis,
and other tribes. It is assumed that the Bhauma-Kara dynasty
was founded by the Bhuiyas. Savara blood flows in the Khurdah
royal family– one of the founding fathers of Khurdah family
married a Savara lady. The Sailodbhava dynasty also bears the
same heritage. It is understood from an inscription that one of
the kings of Kalinga, Pulindasena by name, prayed to Lord Shiva
for an heir. With the boon from Lord Shiva the founding father
of this dynasty came out piercing a part of the Mahendra
mountain *(Shila-sakala-udbedhi)*. The name Pulindasena points to
the aboriginal tribe Pulindas. The kings of Mayurbhanj belonged
to a very old family of Orissa. Legends say that this family's
founding father was born out of a peacock's egg. The peacock
is an important totem of the aborigines. The Sambalpur-Gajrat
area was under the occupation of the Kondhs, for which this
area was known as Kondh-Malika area (Kondh occupied area).
The state of Gangpur was the creation of the Gonds and Bhuiya
landlords. Bhuiyas also established the states of Bonai and
Keonjhar. Stambheshwari was guardian angel of the Bhanjas of
Sonepur-Baudh area during the 9th and 10th centuries. This
Stambheshwari deity was founded there by the Sulkis. In the
5th-6th centuries Sulkis were ruling in the southern part of
Sonepur. At that time one of its kings, Tustikara by name,
founded and started worshipping Stambheshwari. This family for
many years controlled the coastal area of the rivers in
Dhenkanal-Talcher. *Markandeya Purana* narrates that this Soulika
tribe had been living in the area between Kalinga and Chet, i.e.
South Kosala. Mahashivagupta Yayati the First belonged to this
area, and there was Savara blood in his family. During the later
part of the 8th century the then Sulki king murdered Dhekta,
the Savara chieftain of the neighbouring area. According to
Pandit Vinayak Mishra *(Dynasty of Medieval Orissa)* Dhekta is
the legendary Savara king Dhenka, in whose name that area is
known as Dhenkanal. Even now there is a monument at
Dhenkanal for remembering Dhenka, which is revered by the
local populace. After the decline of the Sulkis, the custody of
the deity Stambheshwari passed on to the hands of the Bhanjas.
During the Matharas rule, some parts of western Orissa were
being ruled by the tribal groups known as Nala, Saravapuria,
Stambheshwaripadabhakta, etc.

What impact social and political changes make upon a
society can best be ascertained, if the Savara tribe be taken as
example. In the 1961 census the Savaras were divided into two

ategories– one, Saora, Sahara; and the other, Savaras and
.odhas. This categorisation was necessary to differentiate between
hose who were maintaining their tribal individuality from those
vho merged themselves in the mainstream of the larger society.
Enumeration in the Koraput district speaks of 36,329 as Saora,
nd 17,583 as Savaras. Saoras of south Orissa are again divided
nto various groups like Sudha Saora, Kampa Saora, Kudumba,
.angia or Arsi Saora, Ghunta Saora, and Jara Sabar. Saoras of
he coastal area of north Orissa have merged themselves in the
Hindu mainstream. In fact, almost two-third of the Savara
.opulation have become amalgamated with the Hindus.

That the tribal population was heavily concentrated in and
round the Puri district can also be known from the names of
illages like Bhil Sasan, Bhil Deoli, Bhiligram, etc. From the
vritings of the great Oriya poet Sarala Dasa we come to know
nat, a) Savara kings had been ruling in the Manohar-ban area
ear Puri; b) Kandukakanan near Konark was being ruled by the
iboriginal tribe; c) on the sea coast beneath the Mahendra
nountain, the region known as Trikalagiri was being ruled by
he Savara king Trikalahasti; d) on the south-west of this area
vas Mahendramala, a mighty Savara kingdom, ruled by king
Karunakara; and e) in between Karnata and Maharashtra, an area
vas known as Kirata Desa, whose king was known as Kirata
ena.

In the introductory chapter of this book it has been
nentioned that when Samudra Gupta invaded Kalinga, it was
ivided into small kingdoms, and that these kingdoms, in spite
f their very limited strength, fought with Samudra Gupta.
mportant kings among those were Vyaghraraja of Mahakantara,
Mantaraja of Kurala, Mahendragiri of Pistapura, Mahendra of
Kosala, Swamidutta of Kettua, Damana of Erandapalli, and
Kuvera of Devarastra. From the names of those kingdoms and
aeir kings it can safely be assumed that these areas were
ominated and ruled by the aboriginal tribes. Ethnically, Oriyas
re not of one homogeneous origin. Besides the primitive Odras,
Jtkalas, and Kalingas, the non-Aryan martial peoples like the
avaras, Mundas, Kondhs and others were the dominant
.habitants of Orissa.

There is no two opinion now that before the invasion of
ae Aryans in India, the entire Indian peninsula from the
Iimalayas in the north to Sinhala in the south was dominated
y the non-Aryan Dravidians and the aboriginals. Mohenjodaro,

Harappa and other such places give ample proof that in the pre-Aryan age Indian culture was of a very high standard. And the primitive races were known for their might and zeal in maintaining their independence, for which they could resist the continuous onslaught of the Aryans for several thousand years,and could confine the Aryans within Uttarapatha (northern zone). The primitives had to migrate to the other side of the Vindhyas because of their ignorance of bronze and iron tools, with which the Aryans were conversant, and for their not having any means for quick nanoeuvering in the matter of conveyance, whereas the Aryans had for that purpose their horses. Still, the Aryans had to console themselves for several thousand years with the rule over the area which was known as Uttarapatha, i.e. North India The verses in the *Rg-Veda* are ample proofs of the non-Aryan prowess— in frontal war it was a difficult task to beat these non-Aryans, who are termed as 'dasyus' *(dacoits)*. In these verses Aryans are seen to be inviting their warrior-god Indra and other gods not for any other purpose but for helping them to get control of those *dasyus*' properties, cows and females, which they were in constant need of. However, because the Aryans had to wait for several thousand years to get control of the lower part of the Ganges valley and the southern part of the Vindhyas, they declared those areas, now known as Bengal, Orissa, Andhra, etc., as *Mlechhadesa* (land of the evil people— untouchables). *Aiteraya Brahmana* (800 B.C) admits that the *dasyus* of the Savara origin along with other aboriginals were controlling the borderland of the *Aryabhumi* (land of the Aryans). In the eastern and southern areas of India, dominated by the aboriginals, particular mention has been made in the different *Puranas* and old Sanskrit literature of the Savaras, who are called the *dayitas* (beloved) of the Lord Jagannatha.

CHAPTER III

THE SAVARAS

AMONG THE primitive tribes the Savaras were known to be valorous and independent spirited. Ample proof of their prowess is to be found in ancient Sanskrit literatures, like *Brahmanas*, *Ramayana*, *Mahabharata*, different *Puranas*, *Katha Sarit Sagara*, and in Banbhatta's *Kadambari* and *Harsacharita*. In the *Ramayana* it has been mentioned that on the bank of the river Pampa, at the foot of the Vindhyas in Madhya Pradesh, Ramachandra went to the cottage of an old lady ascetic, who belonged to the Savara tribe, and conversed with her. This incident has practically no significance with the main story of the *Ramayana*. It seems that Valmiki mentioned this small incident with two purposes in mind – I) to indicate that the Savaras were powerful in the Dandaka area, 2) to hint that Hinduism was slowly penetrating among these non-Aryans. Mention of the lady Savara ascetic was just symbolic. In the Hindu scriptures the inhabitants of the south of the Vindhyas have been mentioned as "ferocious Savaras". It was they who repeatedly checkmated the continuing Aryan onslaught. The *Aiteraya Brahmana* has mentioned that these Savara *dasyus*, along with other aboriginals, were dominating the areas on the borderland of *Aryabhumi*. It has also been said that these Savaras were descendants of Vishwamitra, who cursed them to live as impure people. But in the *Mahabharata* it is a different story. It says that when Viswamitra was trying to plunder Vashistha's "wishing cow" Nandini, she, to save herself from abduction, produced a host of *mlechhas* (impure people) from her body. These were Dravidas, Yavanas, Savaras, Kanchis, Paundras, Sakas, Pulindas, Andhras, Keralas, Sinhalese, Barbaras, etc. It should be noted here that those impure people were mostly named after places of India, where the aboriginals were the dominating forces, and most of these places are located in the lower Ganges valley and in territories to the south of the Vindhyas. It indicates that at that remote age the Aryans were not agreeable to treat those aboriginals even as human beings. Anthropologists say that those Savaras belong to the Kolarian group of people, among whom are Bhils, Mundas, Pulindas, Savaras, Hos, Santhals, etc. Their might and indomitable courage for maintaining their independence have been derisively mentioned in Sanskrit literature. In these literature they are objects of scorn, only because they thwarted many attempts of the Aryans to push forward beyond *Aryabhumi*.

In many historical notices Savara chiefs have been mentioned. About 1800/1900 years ago Pliny referred to them as Suari, and Ptolemy as Sarbari. Banabhatta wrote his *Harsacharita* in the first century A.D. He wrote that soon after Harsavardhana had ascended the throne in the year 507, he went to the Vindhya mountainous area in search of his sister Rajyasree, and became friendly there with the mighty Savara king of the area, Bhukampan (literary meaning - earthquake). It seems that this name Bhukampan was symbolic, symbol of the might and valour of the Savara king. Banabhatta in another book of his, *Kadambari,* has described the Savaras as ferocious people. While mentioning the Savara king of Dandakaranya, Matanga, he remarks that "He was as the child of the Vindhya mountains, the partial avatar of death; the born brother of wickedness, the essence of Iron Age" (*Kadambari.* Trans: C.M. Ridding). After a while he admits of the personality, might, high-mindedness of the king, and says that the king draws fear as well as reverence. So, we can conclude that even in the first century A.D. Aryan or Brahmin advancement remained stalled at the north of the Vindhyas. This is the reason for naming the Savaras as "Vindhya Malikas" (Lord of the Vindhyas) in the Puranas. As far as we know Agastya was the first Aryan Brahmin to cross the Vindhyas. It has been mentioned in the Santi Parva of the *Mahabharata* that these Savaras along with other *dasyus* carry on immoral activities.

In the Udayindiram inscription of the Pallava king Nandivarman Pallavamalla, it has been mentioned that during his twentyone year rule he defeated the Savara king Udayana, and the Nishada king Prithwivyaghra. It happened in the year 736 A.D., when after defeating Udayana, Pallavamalla plunderd Udayana's peacock flag that was set with mirrors. From *Epigraphica India* it is known that the western Ganga king Narasimha the Second (963-974 A.D.) defeated one Savara King, Naraga by name.

In the *Rg-Veda* non-Aryan aboriginals have been mentioned a number of times. In verse after verse they have been ridiculed— because of their might and wealth. From these verses we come to know of the aboriginal leader, Sambara, possessing a hundred settlements, Pipru ninetynine, Banasree another hundred; after mentioning these the Aryans are found to be invoking Indra to help them plunder the cows, land, and the females of those *dasyus*. It seems that the Aryans had no idea about the ethnic variety among the Indian aborigines, and as such they were all commonly termed as *dasyus*. Among the early Sanskrit books, the *Aiteraya Brahmana* first listed them into different groups, and since then we come to know of these groups as Savaras, Pulindas, Poundras, Andhras, Keralas, Mutias, etc.

In the historic age we come across many aboriginal royal families in Orissa, some of which have been mentioned before. From the Korni copperplate inscription of the Ganga king Anantavarman Choraganga, we come to know of Kamarnava, the founder of the Eastern Ganga dynasty. In it has been stated that around the year 720 Kamarnava established the Ganga dynasty by defeating and killing Savaraditya, the Savara king of the eastern area of the Mahendra mountain. Whatever that may be, it is now recognised that during the period 800 B.C. to 1200 A.D. the Savaras were the most dominant group among the aborigines of east and central India.

General Cunningham says that from various papers and records it has been found that there were many Savara kings and commanders in the middle ages. In the later period Gond tribe maintained predominance on both banks of the river Narmada in the Vindhyas— the same predominance was maintained by the Savaras in the earlier days. In this connection he stated that "In the Saugar district I was informed that the Savaras had fiercely fought with the Gonds and that the latter had conquered them by treacherously making them drunk". (*Archaeological Reports, No.17,* pp. 120,122).

It has earlier been mentioned that the Savaras belong to the Kolarian group of people. They can be divided into two categories - 1) Hill Saoras, and 2) Saoras of the plains. Among the Hill Saoras there are six clan types - Malia Savar, Arsi or Langiya (who bear monkey totem), Luara or blacksmith, Kindal, Kumbi, and Jadu. Saoras of the plains are divided into two clans - Kapu or cultivators, and Suddha Savara (Savaras who have become pure). These Kapu Savaras follow some traditional customs of the Hill Saoras, but the Suddha Savaras have become Hindus and they have adopted the Oriya language as their own. There is an impression in vogue that the Hill Saoras are masters in the art of magic; this art is known as Savarividya in Oriya language.

Though the Saoras are well spread out in different states of the country, they are concentrated mainly in Madhya Pradesh, Andhra Pradesh, Orissa, and Tamilnadu. Incidentally, it should be

mentioned here that there is another community among th
Savaras, who call themselves as Seori-Narayana Savaras. The
mostly live in the Sambalpur district. This name they hav
derived from the village Seori-Narayana located in the district c
Bilaspur in Madhya Pradesh. It is said that this was the villag
where the aged Savara lady ascetic welcomed Ramachandra i
her hut, when he was passing through the Dandaka region. I
this connection there is a legend very much in vogue which i
being mentioned here. According to the legend, before the Pu
temple was erected Jagannatha used to be worshipped at th
Seori-Narayana village. One aged Savara was looking after an
worshiping the god. The King of Puri plundered this god from
here and installed it in the Puri temple.

This legend will be discussed in detail later on. Thes
Savaras merged themselves completely with the Hindu mainstrean
and they do not even keep any contact with the Hill Saoras.

The Hill Saoras try to maintain the tradition c
rebelliousness and martial prowess for which the Savaras wer
renowned in the early period of their history. They are alway
alert and ever eager to maintain their own freedom an
personality. In social matters they do not have any inhibitio
about caste differences, neither is there any restrictions among:
their womenfolk in regard to their movements etc. These Saora
revere their local chiefs and follow their advice.

In the field of religion, the Saoras have quite a larg
pantheon of gods and goddesses. In general, these gods an
goddesses are taken to be malevolent. Among these deities the
accord prime position to the Sun God, who is named Uyungsu
They think that this Sun God is upright and benevolent, in spi
of their belief that he curses people with the terrible disease c
leprosy when he gets angry.

General Cunningham says, "In Sanskrit savara means
corpse'. From Herodotus, however, we learn that the Scythia
word for an axe was sagaris, and as 'G' and 'V' are inter
changeable letters savar is the same word as sagar. It seem
therefore not unreasonable to infer that the tribe who were s
called took the name from their habit of carrying axes. Now
is one of the striking peculiarities of the Savaras that they a
rarely seen without an axe in their hands. The peculiarity ha
been frequently notced by all who have seen them." (Ibi
p.113).

The tradition that this wild tribe has been trying to maintain for the last several thousand years is now withering away under the impact of modern civilization. Civilization changes with the ages, and this change has many good effects. But the changes have a negative side also : in keeping pace with the modern trends man becomes perplexed and ultimately becomes captive of the institutions that they have created in the process. Shall we then assume that it is because of this negative attitude to change that the Savaras, though they are in miniscule minority, have been knowingly or unknowingly evading its call?

CHAPTER IV

RELIGIOUS FAITH OF THE ABORIGINES

EVERY COMMUNITY has its own religious faith. It is natural that the oldest inhabitants of this country, who are now known as primitives or aborigines, should have their own religious faiths. Just as different sects came into existence in the Hindu religion and these sects adhere to different religious tenets, similarly among the aborigines also, as there are diverse communities, so there are diverse religious creeds. Primitive thought recognised only natural forces that influenced human life and so in primitive man's religious thought imagery of the human being did not find place. In primitive religion basic constituents were trees, animals, rivers etc, and the tree has a special significance. To them the tree is the source of life. Worshipping the tree was a big festival not only among India's primitive people, it was so everywhere in the world among the primitives.

Idolatry and anthropomorphistic ideas have no place in aboriginal thinking. The Baigas consider Nanga Baiga as a human being, but they do not instal any image of their Nanga Baiga. Murias treat their God Linge Pen as the founder of their community, still they do not set up any image of Linge Pen. Marias do not erect any temple for their god Mahapurusa, Godabas, Diadis, Parengas, Jhorias or Bundoras do not set up any image of their gods or goddesses or of their demigods. Santhals too do not model their chief deity Chando (Sun god). In their religious faith, the eastern side is very important, as the Sun god appears from that end. It has been noticed only that the Saoras construct small rude figures in thatched rooms with open sides all round, or in the forests. Their deities are modelled on an urn-shaped pot with motley colours, or in a stone with variegated colours, or on a log or a tree. And in some places they place some ugly and unshapely goblin-like figures. On the roadside of Saora habitations in the mountainous areas of the districts of Ganjam and Koraput a figure made out of a log is occasionally noticed– a tall manlike deformed figure, which, for them denotes a Sahebasum, i.e. a figure of a sahib (European) with a cap on. This figure was imagined out of fear of the Europeans. In fact, out of fear of natural calamities and diseases, they created their gods. To their family life an urn-like pot or a wooden cup is very significant. In their religious faith these pots are treated as very important. To them breaking of such a pot is a very sorry affair. To them land is the temple, cultivable tools and implements are the religious elements. As we are here discussing about the imagery of Lord Jagannatha, it would be proper to discuss the religious beliefs, briefly, of the Savaras only, as it is they who are named as the *dayitas* (beloved) of the Lord.

Saora religious beliefs are very confusing, as they differ according to regions. As this tribe is divided into small disjointed groups, inconsistencies in their beliefs are many and natural. For example, who is the Supreme god– Uyungsun or Ramma-Bimma-Sitaboi? Though, in general, Uyungsun is treated to be the principal god, a few groups do not accord that position to this god. Before discussing this point, we would like to discuss here, in brief, their ideas about 'soul' or 'god'.

Man possesses two souls– Suda Puradan or heart at large, and Sanna Puradan or small heart. Sanna Puradan is also known as Balang Puradan or *Rup-Rup* Puradan. The meaning of the word Balangan is roof of a house. As a room needs a roof life requires a soul, which is the small soul. Puradan means life. The small soul resides in the heart, wherefrom it pulsates *rup-rup* like (light rapping sound). When the small soul disappears from the body, man faces death. The big soul or Suda Puradan has practically no role in maintaining life. It exists even after death. When the living man is asleep, this big soul comes out of the body and rambles in the world. This soul even converses with the god and occasionally enters the underworld for gaining experience. To us what is a dream, to the Saoras it is no dream, but occurrence, a reflection of the experience gained by the big soul.

After the death of a person, the big soul, after leaving the body, becomes at first a shadow, and later on, in course of time, becomes an ancestor. Immediately after the death of a person this soul enters the netherworld for some time, and after the cremation, till the great soul becomes acquainted with the forefathers and till the expensive Guar ceremony is observed, it wanders the world. After this ceremony it enters the underworld and lives with the other ancestors. The ceremony is expensive to them, as a buffalo has to be sacrificed and villagers are to be invited to the feast. But as these people are economically poor, most of the time thay can not hold this ceremony within the due period. But as they believe that with the touch of death the soul gets polluted, and that till the Guar ceremony is performed these souls remain naked and hungry, they try not to delay its observance.

There are categories among the souls living on the other side of the world. Among them the topmost position belongs to the ancestors, i.e. *idaisum* (deified dead). These ancestor-guardians are treated as 'Sonuman' or God. They have been given the names of Sedsum, Mannesum, Radasum etc. Not only do these guardians occupy the highest position, they are also supposed to wield unlimited power, and to enjoy having the best clothes, and the best food in their beautiful houses. These guardians are supposed not only to give companionship to the other dead staying in the other world or in the underworld, they also maintain important contacts with even living persons. Of course, such contacts are maintained through the medium of their Samans (priests). In their thinking the underworld is in the south of this world, east and western sides are the thoroughfares for the movements of the Sun and Moon, and the northern side is the path of the Raingod. The underworld is called by the Saoras as Minorai or Jaitandesh.

Sonuman is the Saora synonym of god. These Sonumanjis are known by different names–some of them are Sky gods, some village gods, and others are particularly malevolent gods, who bestow to human beings all types of troubles. Though all the Kittungs can not claim to be worshipped, in their beliefs Kittungsoms or Kittungs are also gods. To the Saoras, Kittungs are more human like. There are many legends around the Kittungs, who are supposed to be the creators of the universe and upholders of humane activities. In the prevalent Saora legends Kittungs are depicted as heroes.

After the ancestors, the next place is of the guardians, who are also treated as gods. Their importance is more with the priests, as they are supposed to converse through the priests. The last position belogns to the other dead, who are called Kulbanji or shade. Until they can get a place in the assemblage of the ancestors, they are recognised as only shadows. They are not treated as gods.

Again, among the gods only a few have the competence to be worshipped. It should be remembered that in their religious thinking most of their gods possess permanent houses for their living– these houses are located either in the sky, or on the ground, or in the nether world. The great sky gods like

Uyungsun, Darammamesum, Lankasum live in the sky, high above the head. To their thinking the Moon or Angaiboi is the wife of the Sun god, and Ringesum is the air god. The gods who reside on the ground are treated as village or local gods, and these gods are mostly connected with the mountains and rivers. Other ancestor guardians live in the underworld.

There are four types of Saora priests—Buia, Kuranmoran, Edaimaran, and Sigarman. The chief of the village plays the role of Buia priest in the religious activities of the Saoras of the Ganjam district. The Shaman is a holy man to them— these Shamans prescribe medicine and in each animal sacrifice they act as the chief priest. These Shamans are called Kuranmorans. Edaimaran priests help the Shamans in their work and perform small functions during cremation etc, and it is the Sigarmons who perform the obsequies. The cheif of the Buias is called the Sadi Buia. Buias mainly work as the priests, but the Sadi Buias have enormous power, In fact, their position in society is just after the chief of the Saoras.

Saoras do not have faith in reincarnation. They believe that dead persons can not have any rebirth. The dead lives in the sky, on the ground, or in the underworld as ancestors, guardians, or as shadows.

It has been mentioned earlier that among the primitive tribes the Saoras erect some figures for their gods. These are made from logs, and the curvings are rude, unrefined and distorted. But such wooden figures are not found in the mountainous areas, where Hill Saoras reside, as they still follow the old tradition of not carving an image of the deity. For these reasons scholars think that these figures are weak manifestations of Hindu gods and goddesses. But the Saoras think that the Hindus rob them of these deformed figures. A current story in this regard is being narrated here :

In the earlier days prayer houses to worship the Kittungs were erected in the jungles far outside the villages. The prayer house was nothing but an open thatched place. In a Saora village one aged Shaman was living with his wife and daughter.One day a Brahmin from outside came to them and begged shelter, which was afforded to him. After some time the Brahmin put forward to the aged Shaman a proposal to marry his daughter. As the proposal was not in keeping with the scriptural practices, the old man was not agreeable   to it. But the Brahmin continued soliciting eagerly the favour of the Shaman, and ultimately proposed to him that if his daughter was given in marriage with him, the Brahmin will work under him as an employee for seven years. Because of the girl's insistence in favour of the proposal, and the Brahmin's continuous solicitations, the Shaman ultimately agreed to hand over his daughter in marriage with him. After the marriage the Brahmin started helping the old man in many ways, particularly in the matter of worshipping, for which the old man contemplated to hand over all the responsibilities to look after the prayer houses to his son-in-law at the time of his death. Meanwhile the son-in-law had noticed that the old man had been entering the forest to offer food to the Kittung all alone, and he was not allowed to follw him there. And so, the Brahmin started humbly entreating the old man for taking him along in the forest so that he could know the location of the prayer houses. Ultimately, the old man agreed to take him there on condition that the Brahmin will have to remain blindfolded to and from his house and the prayer house. At the time of covering his eyes the daughter of the Shaman stealthily passed on some cotton seeds to her husband and advised him to scatter these seeds on his way to the prayer house. On reaching the prayer house, his eyes were uncovered, when he found that there were two distorted figures—Kittung and his wife. The old Shaman was offering them raw food. After some time when cotton saplings were visible on the way, one day the Brahmin all alone entered the jungle and approached the Kittung with the prayer, "Oh Kittung, the old Saora offers you only raw food. If you come along with me I shall offer you food cooked with milk, sugar and ghee." Soon after the Kittung nodded his approval, the Brahmin stole the figures and ran away to Puri. When this theft came to the notice of the villagers, the Saoras decided that thence forward prayer houses for the Kittungs would be erected only inside the village, and that prayer houses would not contain any figure of the Kittungs. (L.S. Malley,*Census, 1911*).

It is intended to discuss this story in a later Chapter.

There is a Saora legend which explains why the Saoras erected such deformed figures. The legend runs thus :

One day in the Rawangiri mountain Mahaprabhu Kittung broke a stone, from which fire came out. The splinters of the stone hurt the head and the left side of the Klittung, and, not only that, the heat of the fire was so intense that the head and the legs of the Kittungs got burnt. The injury was so severe that thenceforward the Kittung dwelled there as lame and deformed. As because the fire was thus discovered by the Kittung, the Saoras became grateful to him and from then they started to model such deformed figures of the Kittungs for the purpose of worshipping.

Fear is the mother of religion. Unexplainable occurrings like thunderstorm, earthquake, fire, etc. caused fear among the primitives. Not only that, fear of the wild animals, unnatural sounds, all these sowed the seeds of religion. Awe-inspiring incidents frightened the primitive peoples. Truly speaking, fear is the earliest religion in the world. Blind faith in animism is the original form of religion. And this attitude bred the mentality of worshipping the ancestors, adoring the planets, and even worshipping the trees, stones, rivers, and mountains. Indispensable characteristics of religion are those of purity and impurity. As in Hinduism, aboriginals also believe in animism, and with it was added superstition and magic. The sky is the limit and it is far beyond man's reach, and so the invisible occurrings that come down to the earth must be due to some unnatural forces, which remain out of sight. As there was no way then to know the unknowable, the unknowable deserved adoration. This was the thinking not only of the Indian primitives, but also of the Aryans. The ever-glowing Sun in the sky, as manifest in its daily trajectory over the sky, was taken to be the force behind all that happens on the earth. And the Sun became the pre-eminent God to the Kolarian groups of people. The Savaras call this god as Uyungsun, Mundas as Sing Bonga, Khonds as Bura Panu or Bela Penu, and Oraons call it as Dharmesh.

It has been stated earlier that like the Hindus, the Savaras have also a long list of gods and goddesses, though all of them are not regularly worshipped. The thatched prayer houses are erected only for select deities. It should again be mentioned that their deities are mostly symbols of terror and diseases. Contact with Hinduism for hundreds of years has naturally made an impact on their religious beliefs and customs and has brought about certain changes in their life style. In spite of that, those among the primitive tribes who want to uphold their lifelong traditions do not make images of their deities. The symbols of their deities are pieces of log or a tree, or stones, or else ornamented earthen pots ; and their temple is an open space, kept neat and clean, or at best a thatched open hut.

As has been mentioned earlier, to them the supreme Kittung is Uyungsun. There are many Kittungs who are deemed to be the followers of this Sun god, for which whatever offerings these Kittungs get, one part of it goes to Uyungsun. As Hindu gods are named variously, their chief Kittungs are also differently named. The Sun god has different names like Darammasum, Lankasum, Adununkisun, Gadelasum, Marendra-kumsum, Danammaboi, Gadajangboi, Uyungboi. As Uyungsun the Sun god helps the ladies to conceive, as Gadejangboi it helps to construct the bones of the conceived child, and as Darummasum it keeps vigil over all the activities of the human beings. The Sun not only gives life, it also takes it back. When angry it punishes the sinners by cursing them with leprosy and epilepsy. Still, the Sun god is more or less benevolent. There is some controversy among different groups about the supremacy of the Sun god. Those who treat Gallosum or Karnosum or Labosum as the supreme god think that Uyungsun is their adviser. But the majority gives the predominant place to the Sun god, as it symbolises truth and justice, in spite of the fact that it cursed the children with fever and leprosy. Darummasum, i.e. the other name of the Sun, means right-eousness, though it also troubles them by inflicting leprosy and epilepsy. In a Saora legend mention has been made of one Kittung named Mahaprabhu, who has been supposed to be the creator of the Sun (it seems this legend is not very old, because Mahaprabhu was not a Saora word). However, it can be inferred that leprosy was widely prevalent among the primitive tribes, otherwise there would not have been so many deities inflicting people with leprosy.

S.V. Sitapati is of the opinion that there is a supreme deity, which is not clearly defined in the Saora mind. He considers that this deity is the Sun, Uyungsun, who is also known as Darummasum, Lankasum and sometimes as Gadelsum or Gadejongboi (S.V. Sitapati, "the Saoras", *The Journal of Andhra Historical Research Society, Vol. 13*, p.133).

In the Saora legends we come across several other powerful Kittungs, besides the Sun god. Amongst them, mention may be made of two brothers and a sister - Ramma, Bimma, and Sitaboi -. Ramma is the earth, Bimma the sky, and Sitaboi is the symbol of wealth and abundance. In this story these two brothers and the sister are said to be the creators of mankind. In this legend we come across two other Kittungs - Jagannatha

Kittung, who is taken to be Ramma-Bimma incarnate, and Manjorasum Kittung, the Lord of Puri. It should be noted here that the icons of Manjorasum have three deformed figures, two male and one female (similarity with Jagannatha-Balabhadra-Subhadra to be noted).

In the Saora religious beliefs, the place of the body is very important, for which they are ever vigilant to keep the body healthy and clean. Their religious customs and practices centre round the keeping of a healthy body. They become bewildered when a death occurs, as death in the family involves heavy expenditure   the costly Guar ceremony, about which mention has already been made, has to be performed, besides other expenses.   They do not desire that the dead remains homeless, hungry, naked and that it moves around as a shadow. As they believe that death is not the last word, death does not separate the body with their relatives, and, hence, they perform the Guar ceremony.   And because of such faith, they do not believe in reincarnation, as the Hindus do.

It should be noted here that in a Saora society the women occupy high positions, and the women have important functions to perform at the time of cremation. And that there is no caste distinction in their society. Even if somebody is converted to other religious beliefs, which happens regularly, they are not treated as outcastes. As they do not believe in any form of untouchability and caste distinctions, they have no prejudice to take food from any body, of however low origin he is.

It is because of the belief in animism, and in the belief of the Great Soul's living either in the sky or on the ground or in the nether world, that they offer and place with the dead body clothes, food, alcoholic beverage, and such commodities for which the dead had a liking. They put these things with the body under the cover, so that the departed gets its food, clothes, etc. till the Guar ceremony is performed, and that the dead one does not come to trouble them for these things. The Hill Saoras keep a coin or some costly material with the dead body, so that while proceeding to the netherworld or   elsewhere the departed kin does not feel the want of money for his needs. If any Saora is killed by a knife or an iron weapon, they keep an earthen pot containing a piece of iron or an arrow besides the corpse.

To them death is not caused by natural causes, the end

comes because of the anger of the gods, ghosts, and goblins. In short, ghosts, goblins, and malevolent spirits have important place in the religious beliefs of the Savaras and of the other aboriginals.

CHAPTER V

LORD JAGANNATHA AND DIFFERENT RELIGIOUS 'ISMS'

THE EARLY history of Lord Jagannatha is so hazy and confusing because of non-availability of any recorded history, that it becomes difficult to portray a proper picture. Volumes have been written on Orissa's ancient history, but not much has been written on the history of the Lord. Eminent scholars and researchers are, of course, trying hard to reach a definite formulation about the form of the idol of Jagannatha. As a result, though varied theories centring round this form have been enunciated, one important element common to such discussion is that this image of Lord Jagannatha was first shaped by the primitive aborigines, the Savaras. But confusion persists in regard to other details.

It seems certain that the first non-primitive religion that infiltrated into this tribal-dominated area was Jainism in and around 5th century B.C. That Jainism had enough influence in Kalinga can be gauged from the fact that the king Mahapadma Nanda of Magadha occupied Kalinga and he took away therefrom the "Kalinga Jeena" image to Magadha. According to the Jaina devotees this "Kalinga Jeena" image was that of Rishavadeva or of Parswanatha. Pandit Nilakantha Das opines that this Jeena image is in actuality that of Lord Jagannatha. In this connection he wrote that, "Jagannatha is primarily a Jaina institution...This Jagannatha, it appears, was there in the coast of Kalinga as a piece of black stone which was called Kalinga Jina or symbol of Jina in Kalinga. Later on, it was somehow analysed and the analytical name Nilamadhava was given to it. It seems probable that this explanatory move had some connection with the sunyabad or nihilistic theory which developed out of Mahayana and... pervaded all the then philosophies of India. It came to be the ruling theory when definitely a theory of creation was assumed to explain the beginning of the phenomenal universe. A creation really means to make things out of nothing. The maker is also assumed to be a reality, though in fact he is also nowhere or nothing. So the Buddhist philosophies of the Mahayana school, i.e, the school of Buddhism which conceived Buddha as the creator of the universe and the fountainhead of *karuna* or mercy, naturally developed the theory of Nihilism (*Sunyavada* which means "Everything comes out of nothing"). The Jaina symbol, i.e the stone called Kalinga Jina, therefore, under

4

the storess of that theory came to be explained as Nila (black, nothingness), Ma (mother, creative energy) and Dhava (white i.e. the phenomenal universe)." (*The Orissa Historical Research Journal, Vol.7, No.1,* April 1985). In this connection he also wrote that "... all the four images of Jagannatha are made of neem-wood and the image of Sudarsana wheel, called Sudarsana Chakra of Vishnu, which is one of the four images is a pillar-like block made of the same neem-wood.It represents original Dhammachakra of the Jainas and then of the Buddhists, which is again the Zodiacal path of the Sun in ancient times, represented as a wheel."

Though it is not known what was the extent of the influence of Jainism during pre-Kharavela times, it is known that during the time of the mighty king Kharavela, because of his personal desire and efforts, it did expand much. Herein comes the question-was the figure of Lord Jagannatha established then? This point will be discussed at an appropirate place.

The Nanda emperor's Kalinga invasion and his plundering away the figure of Kalinga Jeena from there to Megadha indicates that in those early days of the historic age, the other religious faith in Kalinga, besides Shaktism, that was being followed by the aborigines, was Jainism. At the time of King Asoka's Kalinga invasion a little bit of Buddhist influence was noticeable, as is known from Asokan edict No.13, where it has been mentioned that in Kalinga there were a few Brahmin and Buddhist hermitages Though it is not correctly known from when Brahmin infiltration started in Kalinga, it must have happened before the invasion of Asoka. Though Asoka did not do much personally for the propagation of Buddhism in Kalinga, as the king's religion and as it was patronised by him, Buddhism did continue and expamnded there.

The Buddhist text *Maha Chattarisaka Sutta* says that two tribal representatives of Utkala carried Buddha's message in Orissa. Two brothers, Tapussa and Bhallika of Utkala, became devotees of Lord Buddha and later on went to Ceylon and established a monastery there. It might be that during the time of Buddha a few more were attracted towards Buddhism, but that was not noticeable enough. In fact, after the death of Buddha, during the two Buddhist conventions, held first at Rajagriha and then at Vaishali, nothing is heard of the influence of Buddhism in Orissa. It appears that after the occupation of Kalinga by Asoka, the Buddhist Hinayana faith did make some headway there.

After Asoka's invasion, the most significant event in Orissa was the advent of the King Kharavela, third in the line of the Mahameghavahana dynasty, in Ist century B.C. In the Introduction part of this work elaborate discussion about Kharavela has been made. After Kharavela a black curtain enveloped the atmosphere of Orissa, and no news were available from there. In the meantime Buddhism started spreading there. It has been noticed that during the first few decades of the Ist century A.D. Dantagiri, Toshala, Puspagiri and a few more places were the chief centres of Buddhism. After the relic of the Buddha (Buddha's tooth) was transferred to Ceylon, the importance of Dantapura started dwindling. But Puspagiri's importance continued till at least 7th century A.D. This can be seen from the writings of the famous Chinese traveller Hiuen Tsang. It can also be said that till the time of Harsavardhana (7th century) the influence of the Buddhist Hinayana faith among the people of Orissa was widespread. Otherwise Harsavardhana would not have lodged a complaint with the Nalanda Monastery. He did not like the generosity that the authorities of the Nalanda monastery had been bestowing on the Hinayana group of Orissa. The Buddhist Mahayana faith gained much ground during the first part of the Bhauma-Kara rule. During the 7th-8th centuries, as in other places, Vajrayana type of Buddhist belief, which was close to Tantricism, became powerful. Its influence on the literature and society of that time was naturally manifest. During this period Buddhist scholars of Orissa composed several books in Sanskrit, books related to Tantra. Amongst those scholars mention may be made of Kansupa, Shavaripa, Kuipa, Indrabhuti, and Lakshimikanta.

Religion always takes help of the political power, without which it is difficult for a religious belief to get strengthened; and, for this purpose an unwritten convention between the religionists and political ideologists has been continuing since the ancient times, and it still continues. Though it is true that in the present age the influence of religion on poltical power is shrinking, because of the secularisation of politics, it has still been noticed that a nexus between the religionists and the political power exists. At present religious fundamentalism among various communities is acquiring, it is hoped temporarily, an increasing importance in the politics of the developing and underdeveloped nations. India is no exception. Caste and religion are being used in India by politicians of all hues to further their own, not always idealistic, ends. Indeed, the interests of both the groups – religionists and political power   are almost the same   As political power in early days remained vested with the kings, it was one of his duties to protect and spread his religious beliefs.   And so, the king became the symbol of God. On this point the *Manusamhita* says, "*Mahati Devata Hyesha Nararupena Tisthati*" (7.8). *Naradiya Dharmashastra* prescribes that a Brahmin, a cow, fire, gold, ghee (clarified butter), sun, water, and the king not only have to be revered, they should be worshipped.   *Gautama Dharmashastra* recognises the king as the embbodiment of purity. Following this tradition, the King of Puri was described as "Chalanti Vishnu" (mobile Vishnu).

Mahayana Buddhists propagated that the image of the Lord Jagannatha was really that of the Buddha - Dhamma, Sangha and Buddha manifested in the Trinity.   And that the *Brahmamani* that is placed at the navel of Jagannatha was nothing but a Buddhist relic – the tooth that was brought from Kushinagar to Kalinga.   It should be noted here that the Buddhists believe in relic worship.   But the point is that the tooth of the Buddha was not kept in Kalinga, it was handed over to the King of Ceylon much earlier, who installed it at Anuradhapura for its daily worship.(See chapter "Myths and Legends").   From this we can come to the safe conclusion that the *Brahmamani* cannot be the tooth relic of the Buddha.   The well-known British scholar, A. Cunningham, supported the view of the Mahayanists, and added that this Trinity is an adoption and distortion of the Buddhist Triratna (Buddha,   Buddhism and Buddhist monastery).   In his book The *Bhilsa Topes* he writes, "When restored to its orginal monogrammatic form, the figure of Jagannatha, or the Lord of the Universe, becomes clear and intelligible, but its present uncouth shape has taxed even the ingenious mendacity of a Brahmin to account for ...."(p. 233). To justify this view he observed that - i) From the Triratna sculpture of Sanchi, it can be said that the figure of Jagannatha resembles that of the ancient Buddhist Triratna; 2) Rathayatra of Jagannatha resembles the procession of the Buddha image, as has been written by Fa-Hian.   He states that Col. Skyes has written in the 6th volume of the "Journal of the Royal Asiatic Society" that both these ceremonies occur at the same time of the year; 3) Because Buddhism does not believe in any class or caste distinction, during Rathayatra and other festivities caste distinction is not found in the Jagannatha temple; 4) Hindus believe that the bones of Sri Krishna have been kept inside the Jagannatha figure. It is against all canons of Brahminism to keep a person's bone inside the idol of any god, though such relic worship is current among the Buddhists.

Cunningham, it can be understood, was curious to know why such a crude image was being worshipped by the Hindus, and threfore he did research on it, with the results mentioned in the above para. European scholars like Hunter, Stirling, Fergusson and others could not disagree with his arguments. Even a wide section of the Indian scholars approved of his conclusions. Two other foreign scholars G. de' Alviella in his book *The Migration of Symbols* and Waddel in his book *Buddhism in Tibet* speak otherwise. Alviella thinks that the figure of Jagannatha is the symbol of the Trishula (trident) And Waddel states that he did not come across any such trinity to which Dhamma, Sangha, and Buddha could be related. He also says that although many scholars said that the Buddhist trinity of this type is found ·in India, his careful observations of the Buddhist figures could not find one such.

How far are Cunningham's conclusions tenable ? He admits that there is a faint similarity between the Jagannatha Trinity and the Triratna of Sanchi That is why, no doubt, while discussing the similarity of both these figures, he remarked that the resemblance is not very clear as the figures are distorted. And he stated that the resemblance can he found if the pure and holy figure of the trinity could be imagined. So, he also suggests that for finding the proper resemblance we have to take recourse to fancy. This conclusion is irrational and confusing. The Buddhist traveller Fa-Hsian imagined *rathayatra* of Jagannatha as a procession of Buddhist images ; as a devotee of Buddhism such fanciful thinking was possible for him, perhaps even permissible. It is to be noted that Fa-Hsian did not visit Orissa, and that he saw Rathayatra of Buddha in several places in North India. And Fa-Hsian did not mention the *rathayatra* of Jagannatha in his travel accounts.

From the days of the hoary past, the Sun god was the only God who had been travelling in a chariot throughout the day over the sky, and the idea of *Rathayatra* came from that phenomenon. In India the Sun god's *Rathayatra* is not now heard of;· as because centuries back the Sun god lost the supreme position among the Hindu devotes. *Rathayatra* of Lord Jagannatha is being held in the Bengali month of Asadh (mid-June to mid-July), when the Sun travels from the northern solstice to southern. In Sicily *Rathayatra* of the Sun god is held during the last part of northern solstice. So, there is a similarity. Moreover, during the *Rathayatra* the chariots are placed towards the north, and at the time of *Punaryatra* (return journey) these are placed southward. Does it indicate the time of the Sun's passing the solstice, as has been mentioned above ? It may also be added that since Vedic times charioteering by the gods was recognised. The *Rg-Veda* mentions the chariot of the Sun God driven by seven horses. It has been said that the Sun is the source of boundless energy; he is the guardian deity of all that is moveable and unmoveable (*Apra Dyaba Prithvi Cantarikshan Surya Atma Jagatastusthusasca*). Seated upon a chariot driven by seven horses he traverses the world for radiating light. In spite of the fact that the devotees of Buddhism and Jainism organise *Rathayatras*, it can not be denied that the idea of Sun God's *Rathayatra* is much older. About the Sun's chariot the *Samba Purana* says the the Sun's chariot is the best of all and for the annual movement of the Sun Lord Brahma constructed it beforehand. Chariots for all other gods were constructed later on. In this connection Nagendra Nath Basu writes in the *Vishwakosha*, "The custom of *Rathayatra* is very old. Apart from Jagannatha's *Rathayatra*, the same for many other Hindu deities is in vogue. Apart from that, *Rathayatra* was being held for the Jaina Tirthankaras Parshwanatha and Mahavira, who preceded Buddha. So, there is no doubt that this custom was adopted much before the Buddha's time."

As regards caste distinction it can be said that in the religious beliefs of the Savaras there is no class or caste distinction, and these tribesmen, as the *dayitas* of Jagannatha, hold important positions in the Jagannatha temple. It is very natural that when the Savaras occupied important positions in the temple, no caste distinction should have been observed. Whereas we find that the temple follows caste distinction, which is the end-result of the influence and predominance of the Hindu religionists. Moreover, if, as Cunningham says, it was due to the Buddhist influence caste discrimination is not being observed during the *rathayatra* and other festivities, why this discrimination is being observed during the other days ? And about *Brahmamani* it has already been discussed earlier and also in the Chapter on "Myths and Legends" that it can not be the tooth relic of Buddha. There is no doubt that due to the influence of Tantricised Buddhism its impact was noticeable in the activities of the temple, but Cunningham does not speak of any other

Buddhist relic. Then again, not three but four deities placed on the *ratnavedi,* are being worshipped, whereas Cunningham speaks of the trinity.

The revival of Hinduism started during the time of the Gupta empire, and in the post-Gupta period the Shakta-Shaiva form of religious beliefs became the dominant belief almost everywhere in India. Orissa did not lag behind, and from the 6th century onwards this Hindu religious denomination became dominant, and during the rule of the Kesari dynasty in the 10th and 11th centuries it reached its pinnacle. During this period almost everywhere in Orissa a number of Shiva temples were built, and Bhubaneswar became the city of temples. The famous temples like Lingaraja, Mukteshwara, Rajarani, etc. were built during this dynasty's rule. During the succeeding Ganga dynasty's rule, though the royal patronage to the Shiva-Shakta form of religious beliefs started weaning away, it was still so strong in the minds of the people that it did not wither away like Jainism or Buddhism. In fact, till the 17th century the Shakta-Shaiva belief was the dominant faith of the general public. In the precincts of the Jagannatha temple complex, at the back right-hand side of the main temple, there is a shrine where Goddess Vimala is worshipped. Vimala is the Shakta goddess, and according t the Shaiva-Shakta belief Jagannatha is the Bhairava, "*Vimala Bhairavi Jatra/Jagannathastu Bhairava*". In spite of the Vishnuite supremacy and control over the present day temple activities, Vimala is recognised as "*Peetheshweari*" (Lady of the holy place). The main food offered to Jagannatha is called *Mahaprasada*, but it should be noted that these food offerings becomes *Mahaprasada* only after it has been offered to Vimala. If the offering is not given to Vimala after it has been offered to Jagannatha, it will not be treated as *Mahaprasada*. Not only that, even in this temple complex, which is now known to be the Vishnu temple, every year during the Durga Puja days goats are sacrificed in front of the Vimala temple inside the temple complex. After all, goddess Shakti is no vegetarian.

In his book *Early Stone Temples of Orissa*, D.Dehejia has remarked that except for a few, most of the early temples in Orissa are Shiva temples, and that there are only two Vishnu temples, six temples of Mother goddess, one Buddhist monastery, and one Jaina monastery. He has also remarked that from the earliest times Shakti faith was being lauded in Orissa. One particular characteristic of Orissa's religious history is that though the kings were followers of one particular religious stream, they were liberal to other faiths, and that there is practically no report of serious conflict in Orissa between different religious groups. The Shaivite king Dhemaraja of the Sailodbhava dynasty gifted land to the Jainas.   King Balarjuna of the Soma dynasty was a devotee of Shiva, but his mother was an ardent Vishnuite. The early kings of the Bhauma-Kara dynasty were Buddhists. From different carvings it is known that king Kshemankara was Vishnuite, his son Sivakara was a Buddhist, and third king was a Shaivite.   From the Royal Charter it is known that though the kings were Buddhists, they helped in erecting Hindu temples. The religious-minded Buddhist king Suvakaradeva's wife Madhavi Devi founded a Shiva temple at Jajpur.   They also contributed much to the maintenance of these temples.   From the Hindal copper plate of Suvakaradeva it is known that for the proper upkeeping of the image of Lord Vaidyanatha in the Pulindeshwara temple, he not only offered the village Noddilo along with the river and the forest of the area, he also authorised them to collect taxes from the villagers.   From the Senakapat stone inscription it is known that the King Balarjuna of the Soma dynasty called himself "Paramamaheshwara" (devotee of Shiva).   Dr Harekrushna Mahtab remarks that Bhauma-kara rulers were very liberal to other religious beliefs, and he has mentioned that at that time the influence of Tantricism was also noticeable.   It has earlier been said that the King Kharavela was also very liberal to other religious beliefs.

The influence of the primitive form of Shakta religious belief, not only in Orissa but all over India, can not also be denied. It commenced its journey in most ancient days.   It will not be wrong to assume from the Mother goddess images found in Mohenjadaro that this belief had its root in the pre-Vedic age.   Archaeological findings confirm that this belief is of pre-historic times.   The Harappan culture has also confirmed this. The changes in the form etc. are only due to the evolution of time.   For this simple reason it can not be doubted that Shakti Puja was in vogue in Orissa before the arrival of Jainism and Buddhism, of course in its primitive form.   The influence of Shaktism on the matriarchal non-Aryans is very natural. The Hindu goddesses Durga, Kali, etc. of the present day were known to those non-Aryans as Savari, Kiratini, etc. though the image-forms were very different.   *Harivamsha* (3/7) narrates that non-Aryans like Savaras, Pulindas, etc. had been worshipping this deity in the forests. *Devi Purana* also confirms this.   Why only the primitive non-Aryans like Savaras, even in Hindu minds, in spite of varied religious influences, reverence for the Mother goddess remains rooted.   As a result, as in other places, in Orissa also, other religious communities has to come to an understanding with Shaktism.   Apart from Tantricised Buddhism, another example is constituted by the customs followed in the Jagannatha temple.   Accepting Vimala as the Lady of the Holy Place, offering the consecrated food of Jagannatha to Vimala before calling it as *Mahaprasada*, sacrificing goats before Vimala in the temple complex are outstanding illustrations of such understanding.

Gods like Indra, Varuna, Agni and Rudra started appearing when patriarchal Aryans came to control society.   Female deities had no important positions.   Mother goddesses were not competent enough to participate in the offerings of *Soma*, A.A. Macdonald says in his book *Vedic Mythology* that in Vedic belief, the place of female deities was in the lowest category.   As a result of continuing confrontation between Aryan and non-Aryan beliefs, the worship of Mother goddesses in different forms and attires got admitted into Vedic society.   Firstly, the Aryans admitted in their pantheon non-Vedic goddesses like Ambika, Durga, Kali, Uma, after which they started searching for their companions (husbands).   The goddess Ambika was first thought of as the sister of Rudra (*Vajsaneyi Samhita White Yayurveda*), but later this Ambika was made wife of Shiva (*Taittiriya Aranyaka*).   On the same model the non-Aryan Shiva was also accepted as one of the chief gods, one among the Trinity - Brahma, Vishnu, Maheshwara, i.e great god Shiva.   In this connection it would not be out of place to state that the Mother goddess is even recognised by the Mahayana Buddhists.   The non-Aryan goddess Nagna Savari, Kiratini, who are called Kali, Durga in the Hindu faith, is known as Parna Savari to the Mahayana Buddhists.   In this process Shaktism secured place amidst Hindu religious beliefs. With various faiths and legends in the field, Shaktism, for all practical purposes, occupied the supreme position in the Hindu religious faith, and its foundation was so strong that still now its influence is uppermost. .   According to the archaeological findings it is known that from 2nd-3rd century B.C Shaktism started influencing the minds of the people of Orissa.   It has been earlier stated that the images of seven Mother goddesses have been found in many places in Orissa. Jajpur is known as Viraja-Kshetra (Land of Goddess Viraja). Apart from the image of Viraja, carvings of many other images of Mother goddesses have been found there. On the banks of the Markandeya tank in Puri images of seven Mother goddesses are there, and on both sides of these images are that of Birabhadra and Ganesha, which are even now being regularly worshipped.

Stambheshwari is the goddess of the aborigines in Orissa – it is nothing but a replica of the Shakti image. A piece of log is the figure of Stambheshwari. Here it may be mentioned that in Orissa goddesses who are widely worshipped are Durga, Kali, Chamunda, Viraja, Vimala, Mangala, Mahisamardini, and Varahi. Indeed, Shakti is being worshipped in almost every family in Orissa either in a recognisable form or in a shapeless form. The main focus of Orissa's culture, however; is on Jagannatha, which is taken to be the Bhairava by the believers in Shaktism-Shaivism, and Vimala is his Bhairavi. In the daily *mantra* (hymns) for worshipping Jagannatha, many tantric rituals are indispensable. In spite of the control and influence of Vaishnavites in the temple since Ganga rule, not only in the temple itself but also in the minds of the people, like Shaktism, Shaivite beliefs are deeply rooted. To the Oriyas, specially to the inhabitants of Puri, the popularity of Lokanatha Shiva is no less. In fact, it is common practice among the general public to call a person, who is suspected to have committed an offence, to Lokantha Shiva, where he is asked to place his hands on the deity and to admit his guilt, if he has committed it. Their inherent belief is that if the person tells a lie, the snake of the Lord will bite him. Of course, this practice is limited to the common folk of Puri.

During the later part of the rule of the Sailodbhava dynasty, Sasanka, king of Karna Suvarna (Bengal), occupied quite a big portion of Orissa. Sasanka was known to be a vehement anti-Buddhist, and he oppressed them very much. Hiuen Tsang has described this in his diary. He stated that though there were some Buddhists in the Odra part of Orissa, they were almost extinct in the Kalinga and the Kongoda parts. It is said that it was King Sasanka who founded the Lingaraja temple at Bhubaneswar. Later on, the Kesari dynasty built on it the present temple.

From diferent inscriptions we come to know that during the rule of the Matharas, Viaishnavism started infiltrating into Orissa. Whether it could enter Orissa before that period is not known due to dearth of materials, though a few scholars think that Vaishnavism had come to Orissa earlier. What we know is that it came to stay there after Samudra Gupta's invasion of Orissa. From the different copper plate inscriptions left by the Matharas dynasty, it is known that the kings were Vishnuites, and they built several temples for worshipping the god Narayana. When the Matharas were trying to propagate Vaishnavism in Kalinga, at that time the Nala dynasty and the Saravapurias in West Orissa became followers of Vishnu. In the history of Orissa's religion we find that post-Matharas rule brought in changes. The royal power came in the hands of the Shaivites, because of which the influence of Vishnuism got reduced. Sailodbhavas and the early Gangas were Shaivites. King Anantavarman Choraganga, who converted himself to Vaishnavism and did much for its propagation, was originally an ardent Shaivite. In the Sellade copper plate of 1084 he declared himself aa "Parama Maheshwara" (devotee of Shiva); in the Korni copperplate of 1112 he declared himself as "Parama Maheshwara, Parama Vaishnava Parama Bhagavata" (devotee of Shiva and Vishnu). From all this it can be understood that till 1112 he did not want to keep himself bound by a particular religious belief, though Vaishnavism was then having an expanding influence. It was in the Vishakhapatanam inscription of 1118 that he ultimately declared himself as only "Parama Bhagavata"(devotee of Vishnu). So, we can conclude that in and around 1118 he finally determined his religious philosophy.

As stated earlier, Vaishnava religious beliefs came to stay put in Orissa during the Ganga rule. It is said that under the influence of the Vaishnava saint Ramanuja, Choraganga became a Vaishnavite. Under the royal patronage this belief ultimately became all-embracing in the Jagannatha temple. And the religious belief that controls the temple activities spreads its influence over the general public. From the archaeological findings and from various available inscriptions we have found that till the tenth century this religious faith was not at all influential nor could it spread out well. As had already been stated, during the pre-Gupta era, except in the southern part of Kalinga, the existence of Vishnuism in Orissa is not known. It entered Orissa from the southern and western part of Kalinga, and its advancement was very slow. From different stone inscriptions it is known that in the 1st century B.C. this religious tenet crossed the Vindhyas and stayed put in the Deccan, and in the 2nd century, A.D. it spread out in the Krishna valley and in south-west Andhra Pradesh. It got royal patronage for the first time when the Matharas and the Pitribhaktas were rulling over a part of Kalinga, in the south of the Mahendra mountain. The Matharas king Ananta Shaktivarman took the title of "Kalinga-dhipati" (Lord of Kalinga), and extended the boundary of his kingdom. From his Andhravaram copperplate inscription it is known that he declared himself as "Narayana-Swami-Padabhakta" (devotee of Lord Narayana). Due to the decline of this dynasty the progress of this religious faith got halted, as after them Kalinga was ruled for 600 years by the Shaivites.

During the rule of the King Harsavardhana, who himself was a Buddhist, in the first part of the seventh century, several Brahmins immigrated to the Toshali area of Orissa. From the Patiakella plate it is known that 37 Brahmins settled in a village in South Toshali, out of whom six were presumably Vishnuites. This village was donated by the then king Sivaraja of South Toshali. Shivaraja was a Brahmin and a Shaivite. During the Gupta rule a group of Vishnuites settled in Raipur and near about places in Kosala (presently, Madhya Pradesh). During the later part of the 6th century, the Vishnuite Nala dynasty was ruling over the districts of Koraput and a part of Kalahandi. After defeating the Nala dynasty in the 7th century another Vishnuite dynasty, the Saravapurias, took over the control of South Kosala. After them this area was ruled by the Pandu dynasty, who were also Vishnuites. During this period Vishnu was being worshipped as Purushottama. So we find that this religious faith, with the help of the smaller kings, entered initially in the southern and western part of Orissa, and later on slowly but steadily extended itself to Central Orissa, and ultimately to the whole of Orissa. The royal patronage that was accorded to Vaishnavism during the Ganga rule continued for a pretty long time. It was under the influence of the Vaishnava saints, Jayadevaa, Ballavacharya and Sri Chaitanya, that Jagannatha became known and worshipped as Sri Krishna. In the religious history of Orissa Sri Ramachandra or Sri Krishna were not earlier much heard of. The images that were being worshipped then by the Vishnuites were those of Lakshmi-Narayana.

We have not yet come across any deity in the history of India's religious beliefs, where so many different theological tenets were intimately involved. In this respect this is a peerless and extraordinary deity, centring which all the religious canons of India, whether it is primitive, or Jaina, Bauddha, Solar, Ganapatya, Shakta, Shaiva or Vaishnava credence, merge themselves in it. Apart from religious beliefs, all the devotional philosophies—Sankara and his monism, Ramanuja and his modified monism, Ramananda and his devotional dualism, Nimbarka and his idea of natural and simultaneous diversity and unity of God and the Soul, Vallavacharya's concept of spiritual growth, Chaitanya's ecstatic humanism—all these got mixed up around this deity.

Idle beliefs, in course of time, becomes national sacraments

nd we accept those as facts of life. Such beliefs characterise
he metaphysical side of Indian civilization. That is why a saying
s in vouge here that "Not reasoning but faith and faith only
eads one to destination. " This mental habit of excessive
lependence on faith was not a quick acquisition but a legacy
anded down from the distant past. The leaders of various
eligious groups exploited this Indian mentality of over-dependence
n super- naturalism. Because of this, scientific and rational
hinking could not find its due place here. Instead of dissecting
omething with the scientific and rational outlook, we are still
he carriers of a mentality which can be called the mentality of
raditional servitude. Let us take the case of Jagannatha of Puri.
here has been much controversy about the origin of this
mage—whether it was a Savara deity, or Kaling Jeena of the
ainas, or Triratna of the Buddhists, Bhairava image of the
hiva-Shaktas, the image of Lord Narayana of the Vishnuites of
Ramanuja. brand, or else Sri Krishna of Jayadeva and Sri
Chaitanya. What we notice is that every religious group
roclaimed this deity as their own, and to make their assertions
videly acceptable, they concocted various types of myths and
egends, which are very many indeed. If the authencity of these
nyths and legends is seriously considered, they turn out to be
ollow. Actually these are the attempts of the religionists to sift
iction in to facts. To win a kingdom and preserve it, political
ower and dogmatic ideologies take resort to continuous
alsehoods, to hoodwink the people, to confuse them, and so to
ead the so-called "mass" like a flock of sheep. And in our
ountry the mass is very much susceptible to these falsehoods.
n their earlier days the various religious faiths resorted to these
actics. The present day political leaders are, in fact, the true
uccessors of those earlier preceptors. We are still struggling with
idgetiness to keep afloat in this situation, and are in the vortex
f complex forces. It has been stated earlier that there is an
nwritten bond between the religionists and the politicians. What
e see today is that innumerable God-incarnates are roaming
ver the country and carrying on propaganda on commercial
asis, whereas our 'democratic' government, holding high the flag
f modernity, knowing very well all the nuisance values created
y these self-made *avataras*, keep mum and allow them to
ontinue their nefarious activities in the name of religion and
od. We are secularists indeed ! As with the help of fantasies,
eligionists wanted to make their followers impotent and paralytic
or the sake of their own interests, so the people who run the
overnment give such latitude to these god-incarnates for the
ame purpose. After all, they are good vote-catchers. Only a

truly secular government will aspire to seeing that people become
rational and take recourse to scientific thinking. Excessive faith
and confidence in supernaturalism is in our atmosphere, because
of which we are reluctant to admit rationalism in our mental
processes. We ignore the truth that to become modern we have
to be rational.

In the Chapter on "Myths and Legends", which follows, the
wellknown stories about Lord Jagannatha will be discussed. Only
the Vishnuite and Buddhist legend, that are in vogue now, will
be described there. As the earlier stories before the supremacy
of Vaishnavism have lost validity now, there is no use dilating
on these. The story in currency is in actuality an admixture of
several such. There was no problem in admixing as the subject
matter does not change qualitatively. Whatever the changes, these
are in names of the characters and in certain minor and
unimportant matters. A spell of illusion has been manifested
around the story in the *Skanda Purana, Padma Purana, Kapila
Samhita, Niladri Mahodaya, Madala Panji, Deul Tola*, Musali
Parva part of Sarala Dasa's *Mahabharata* and several other
books. The scholars have expressed doubts about the historicity
of the *Madala Panji* (chronicles kept in the Jagannatha temple),
and it can be proved that facts are more often fancies. It has
given a chronicle of the kings of Orissa, starting with
Yudhisthira in 3001 B.C. According to it. Yudhisthira ruled for
12 years, Parikshit for 731 years, Janamejaya 551 years, and in
this fashion reaches Vikramaditya and Sakaditys for 135 years till
78 A.D. Let us here discuss the chronicle a little. It does not
mention the name of Asoka, nor that of the King Kharavela,who
brought Orissa to the pinnacle of glory. It can be understood
that as Asoka and Kharavela were a Buddhist and a Jaina
respectively, they are not treated as Hindus and have, therefore,
been omitted. It records that during 538 and 421 B.C., when
king Vajranava Deva was ruling, Mughals and Pathans from
Rajasthan invaded the country; the invasion was, of course,
checked. Soon after one Seiyat Khan from Delhi invaded Orissa,
which was also checkmated. Is it not ludicrous and comical to
believe that in the 5th-6th century B.C. Mughals and Pathans
invaded Orissa? Hallucination or what ? Then it narrates that
during 421-306 B.C. during the rule of Narasimha Deva, Yavanas
from Kashmir invaded his kingdom, and during 306 B.C. and
184 B.C his son Manakrishna Deva checked the invasion of the
Mughals from Kashmir. After that it notes that in 323 A.D.
when a group of Yavanas attacked Puri from the seas, King
Nirmalys Deva fled along with the holy image, and since that

time till the 5th century the holy image lied under the earth. In 474 A.D. King Kesari defeated the Yavanas and freed Orissa from their yoke. He searched for the holy image and could but recover it only after intensive exploration. He placed the idol in the Puri temple. Actual history gives a different version. It says that Kesari kings were on the throne of Orissa in the 10th Century, and that during circa 474 Matharas dynasty was ruling over Puri. Contradictions and confusion thus abound. It can be presumed that such fantasies were the outcome of conflict between different religious faiths.

Whereas they found it offensive to name the Jainas and the Buddhists, they could indulge in the fantasy of bringing in Mughals and Pathans in those days of the hoary past. While discussing this subject, Rajendra Lal Mitra, in the second volume of his book *The Antiquities of Orissa*, remarked that there was an old Hindu adage which says "they rather be eaten up by tigers than seek shelter in a Jaina temple". What malignity towards another religious faith! While discussing this aspect Dr Harekrushna Mahtab in his book *History of Orissa* remarks that it has been proved beyond doubt that whatever has been recorded in the *Madala Panji* is totally false. He also says that it can be concluded after verifying the inscriptions that the *Panji* was written during the Ganga rule. *Madala Panji* also records that the idols were kept hidden in the Chilika Lakes area thrice, wherefrom in 1558 A.D. Yavana commander Kalapahada recovered the image, and that he carried the idols on the back of an elephant to the bank of the Gangas in Bengal, where these were burnt, and as the flames were rising the hands and legs of the Mussalman commander Kalapahada became detached from his body and he expired. The invasion of Orissa and Kalapahada's plundering of the Puri temple are historical facts, and history does not accept the version that his limbs were detached from the body or that he faced instant death. From another story it is known that Kalapahada cremated the idol on the banks of the Chilika. One Bisar Mohanty could get hold of the *Brahmamani* of the idol, which did not get burnt, and brought it to his home for worshipping it there. Later on, at the instruction of the king Ramachandra Deva the *Brahmamani* was brought back to Puri and was again placed at the navel of the idol. As the *Panji* is full of such fanciful stories, there is no need of any further discussion about it.

As in the case of the expansion of a kingdom, so in the spreading out of a religious belief, a tough attitude for achieving the end does not in all cases yield result. Hinduism cannot be said to be a pure Aryan concept. It is still here because of its eclecticism and tolerance and an attitude of compromise. Only when it felt itself seriously cornered by Buddhism, did Brahminism take recourse to compromise, for its own survival. It should be mentioned here that it was because of taking a similar attitude by the Aryans in the early days with the non-Aryans that the former could keep their control over the country. It is true that for such compromises Brahminism had to abandon many of their rites and beliefs and accept and accommodate many non-Aryan and Dravidian customs. Examples– accepting the system of *puja* instead of Vedic *yajna* or sacrifice; deities of the primitive peoples and of the Dravidians being accorded places in the Hindu pantheon of gods and goddesses; accepting Gautama Buddha as an avatara (god-incarnate) etc. In these days of science and technology many changes are happening and are bound to happen, which will have serious impact on society, resulting in changes in religious beliefs also.

For winning and maintaining a kingdom the rulers have to depend on the cooperation of the populace, irrespective of caste-class-colour or religion. They resort to arms only when they feel that diplomatic means are not yielding any result. As the ruling power was vested in the king, it was his responsibility to safeguard and extend his religious beliefs. And for this reason the Hindu scriptures termed the kings as the human symbol of god. It has already been said that the kings of Orissa were termed as "*Chalanti Vishnu*" (mobile Vishnu). In spite of the fact that the security of the religion was invested in the hands of the kings, to maintain their rule they were in need of soldiers, who were recruited from the general public. In the Shantiparva of *Mahabharata*, while giving advice to Yudhisthira, Bhisma told him that an essential element of religion is strength, that is armed forces, and that these forces will give security to the king as well as to the religion of the king. For the same reason, primitive aborigines could not be disowned by the kings of Orissa, rather they were pampered. These people were not only in majority, they were courageous and mighty. These primitives were in all actuality like the armour of the kings of Orissa. As the kings of Orissa mostly came from outside, they had more reason to depend on these tribes— Savaras, Odras, Khonds, Gonds and others for strengthening their armed forces. That these tribes were every mighty can be understood from Asoka's Kalinga invasion, and from Kharavela and other kings' winning extensive kingdoms through wars. As the allegiance of the Savaras and other tribes, who were very much independent-spirited and courageous, was absolutely essential to the kings, and they, for diplomatic reasons, accepted their deities and revered these with all solemnity. It was a master stroke of diplomacy on the part of the kings. The kings not only accepted these deities as their own, they also agreed to give a rightful place to the Savaras in performing the daily rituals in the temple.

Yayati Kesari has been given a place in the *Madala Panji* only because he was able to build up the foundation of Hinduism on a solid basis in Orissa, after stalling the forward movement of the two non-Hindu religions, Jainism and Buddhism. By accepting the aborignial deity as his god, he could also open up the way to bring in the Savaras into the Hindu fold. That his diplomacy yielded result is established from the succeeding history of Orissa. About the image that was interred in the earth at Sonepur in Western Orissa during the Yavana invasion (ref: *Madala Panji*), Yayati Kesari lamented soon after he occupied the throne, "Where is the God?". In search of this god he went to Sonepur and after intensive search he could recover broken parts of the image beneath a tree in village Sapali. He then proposed to erect a new image in place of the heavily damaged and fragmented figure that was recovered there. And for this purpose he invited the Savara carpenters and priests from South Kosala, to which place they were supposed to have migrated at the time of the Yavana invasion, for modelling the image and for arranging its regular *puja*. He also erected a temple for the Lord. From all the accounts and legends it is surmised that Yayati Kesari was the king who was termed as Indradyumna in the legends. But why Indradyumna, and not Yayati Kesari? Firstly, because Yayati Kesari was a devout Shaivite, and the popular legends were written by the Vaishnavites; and secondly, to keep the facts hidden chroniclers at that time were mythomaniacs and they created the mythical Indradyumna. During that time Vaishnavism was not prevalent in Central Orissa. *Brahmanda Tantra*. composed in 1052, mentioning *Rudramala Tantra*, says "*Odrasu Vimala Saktira Jagannathstu Bhairava*" (Vimala of Odra is Shakti and Jagannatha is her Bhairvav). It means that legends in currency were written in the post-Yayati period. It should be mentioned here that from archaeological evidences and from different inscriptions no mention of any religious beliefs centring round Jagannatha is available.

CHAPTER VI

MYTHS AND LEGENDS

IN THE pantheon of Hindu gods and goddesses peculiar characteristics are found in the imagery of Jagannatha— unconventional and special type of an image; no limbs, no ears no shoulder; the body is upto the navel; large bizarre eye without any brows; a massive square head and whatever part o the hands is there, these are separately inserted. At first sigh it looks like a stump of wood, ornamented with colours, with the face and eyes painted on it. Among the Hindu gods and goddesses there are images, both of terrible and frightful type a well as of types which indicate assurance of safety (benevolence) But of whatever type the image may be. it is always artistically carved. Even the Shivalingam (phallus of Shiva), which cannot be called a figure, is artistically done, whereas the style o primitive circular drawing is apparent in the image of Jagannatha Another characteristic is that it is made of wood, the neem (melia azadirecta). The neem wood is not held in such respec by the Hindus as are the banyan, pipul, marmelos, basil (tulasi or mango tree. And Hindu idols are made of stone or clay No evidence is available of any other Hindu god or goddess being made of wood, before Jagannatha idol was curved.

In the pujas and rituals Brahmins are supreme— the las word among the Hindus will be the Brahmin's. But here in this Jagannatha temple in the daily pujas and succeeding ritual a very important position has been given to the non-Hindu primitive tribe, the Savaras, who are not accepted among th Hindus as Jalchal (belonging to a caste whose touch does no pollute water to be used by the Brahmins and other upper cast Hindus). These Savaras are accepted as the dayitas (beloved) and relatives of Jagannatha. Practices during the pujas are also slightly different from those of the Hindus. Throughout the day food is offered to this deity seven times, and that consists o 56 types of palatable dishes. Activities in front of the deit start from dawn. The daily programme is like this— hourl changing of clothings, brushing the teeth, bath in perfumed wate siesta in the afternoon, performance of music and dance b devadasis (women dedicated to the service of the god— th practice is not in vogue now) after dinner in the night befor going to the bed, etc. Royal arrangement indeed ! Such ritualisr is not found in the Hindu practices of worshipping the deities. Exception, if any, is there only in the case of *pujas* to Lord Krishna, but even then that is not so elaborate. We do not know since when such ritualism started. This much is known that music and dance by the *devadasis* was started by King Prataparudra Deva. But it can be presumed that such kind of ritualism is the after-effect of the influence of Vallabhacharya, Jayadev, and Sri Chaitanya, more particularly of Jayadeva and Vallabhacharya among the priests and the kings.

Another noteworthy aspect is that Jagannatha is not all alone; he is accompanied with three other figures on the platform. As is in vogue now, three other figures are those of Balabhadra (elder brother of Jagannatha, i.e. Sri Krishna), Subhadra (sister of Sri Krishna) and Sri Sudarshana (wheel of Sri Krishna). Sri Sudarshana is just a piece of log, dressed in clothes. The two other figures are also distorted and incomplete like that of Jagannatha. The difference lies in the shape of their heads and in the colour of their bodies, and Subhadra does not have any semblance of hands. The very look of these figures is primitive.

To have constructed such on unnatural image and made it acceptable in society of Hindu gods and goddesses must have meant much doing indeed. The best way to do such a thing was through extensive and intensive propaganda and through the media of myths, legends, and exaggerated stories. Not only Hinduism, all religions in the world have resorted to creating such myths for establishing their religious beliefs in the minds of the people. The upholders of all the religions necessarily took resort to creating fantasies and unreal stories. The *Purana* type of books appeared, and these were trumpeted as history. Hindus have implicit faith in the *Ramayana*, *Mahabharata* and the *Puranas* as history pieces, which are not so, though materials for history can be found in these stories. Continuous propaganda for centuries has made the Hindu minds amenable to belief in falsehoods and fantasies.

As it was in the case of religion, so during the present days it is the case with different political ideologies, which spread their tentacles wide and deep with the help of deceptive stories and illusions. As governmental machinery is no longer controlled by the church or temple, closed-system political ideologies have crept in to fill the vacuum created by the separation of religion from governmental power. Religion and politics are inextricably related. One has replaced the other, but the methods of hoodwinking the people to mortgage their brains remain the same. Freedom demands that people should be fearless, without which they are not able to fruitfully participate in building up the country. But the creators of religious and political fantasies attempt to mould mass mentality in such a way through utopian and motivated stories, that people remain timid and awe-stricken. Only the dauntless can help in furthering the spirit of independent thinking. And in the field of independent thinking there is no place for negative and false stories. From ancient times to the present day, the priestly class and now the fanatical political ideologues have, with the help of the ruling powers, succeeded in distorting through falsehoods and baseless fantasies the free fabric of society, so that the spirit of free thinking can not raise its head—free thinking which will be inimical to their interests. Hence, dogmatic political ideologies have now become, in reality, religious ideologies.

As the idol of Jagannatha was not originally a Hindu conception, the Hindu rulers and the priestly class, for maintaining their vested interests felt the necessity of sanctifying it by fabricating and propagating extensively myths and legendary stories about it. Here it may be noted that all this was mostly done in their zeal to popularise this idol as that of Vishnu or Sri Krishna. The current stories are all creation of the Vaishnavites. The Buddhist story is also being mentioned here, as that is of a differnt type, and as the Buddhists claim that the *brahmamani* is the tooth relic of the Buddha. As all the Vaishnavite authors came to almost the same conclusion, whatever may be the *inter se* differences between them, the story that is very much in vogue now is being narrated here. Dissection and analysis of such stories are also essential to find out their inner meaning, which has been done in the later part of this Chapter.

BUDDHIST STORY

It is known from the book *Dalada Vamsha* written by Mahathera Dhammal Kitty in the Sinhalese language that the tooth of the Buddha was transferred to Ceylon from Kalinga. The book has been translated into Pali under the name of *Danta Vamsha*. The book was written in 301 B.C., soon after the so-called tooth relic reached Ceylon. After the death of the Buddha, the monk Kshema Thera brought one tooth from Kushinagar to Kalinga as a relic, and handed it over to the then King of Kalinga, Brahmadatta, for its safe and proper custody. Brahmadatta installed it at Dantapura, the then capital of Kalinga. Sometime after, when Kalinga was being ruled by Guhashiva, it came to be known that one of the kings of Malava intended to plunder the relic. At that time Kalinga was a vassal state of Panduraja of Pataliputra. The belief in the supernatural power of this relic was so widespread that Panduraja was attracted to it, and he requested king Guhashiva to carry the relic to Pataliputra. As there was a possibility of invasion from Malava, Guhashiva being anxious of the safety of the relic took it to Panduraja. Panduraja became convinced of the supernatural power of the relic and was converted to Buddhism. Meanwhile, Kshiradhara, king of Malava, got the information about the shifting of the relic and decided to invade Pataliputra for appropriating the relic. Because of this threat of war Panduraja returned the relic to Guhashiva. At that time a prince from Ujjain came to Kalinga with the purpose of worshipping the relic. While staying in Kalinga, Dantakumar, the Prince, fell in love with Hemamala, daughter of Guhashiva. In the war with Panduraja King Kshiradhara of Malava got defeated and he returned to Malava, when he heard that the relic was back again to Kalinga. Though defeated, Kshiradhara did not give up hope of acquiring the relic. Getting this information, King Guhashiva, desirous of the relic's security, established contact with King Mahasena of Ceylon, and entrusted the responsibility of the safe transferrence of the relic to Ceylon to his daughter Hemamala and son-in-law Dantakumar. When they reached Ceylon Kirtisrimegha (Meghavarma), son of Mahasena, was on the throne, as Mahasena had passed away in the meanwhile. Meghavarma accepted the relic with due reverence and arranged to consecrate it at the temple of Anuradhapura. Fa-Hsian has recorded in his travel diary that he saw the tooth relic then (5th century A.D.) in Ceylon.

In the eighth century when the king of Sambal, Indrabhuti, proclaimed that the idol of Jagannatha was that of Buddha, he announced that the tooth relic of the Buddha was kept inside the idol. At that time the idol was being worshipped inside a cave in the Kot Simlai mountain near Sonepur. Only one tooth of the Buddha was kept as a relic, which was first brought to Kalinga, and then it was shifted to Ceylon in the fourth century. So, the proclamation of the king of Sambal in the 8th century was nothing but a fabrication. It can be well presumed that as the King Indrabhuti was a Buddhist, he tried to publicise such story to make the idol popular at that time. But now the question that comes in the mind is that when in the eighth century Jagannatha was being worshipped inside a cave in the Kot Simlai mountain, can the existence of Jagannatha at Puri at that time be accepted ? The matter will be dealt with at the appropriate place

HINDU STORY (VAISHNAVITE)

It has already been said that for propagating the idea that the idol of Jagannatha is that of Vishnu—Sri Krishna, several stories were circulated. As the central theme of all the stories is essentially the same, there is no need of narrating all these here. Whatever differences there are in the details, these do not affect the main story. The only exception is that whereas in the *Mahabharata* of Sudramuni Sarala Dasa bias is noticeable in favour of the Savaras, the favouritism of the others is for the Brahmins. The story that is now widely current is being narrated here; this is, in fact, a compromised version of most of the stories.

Sri Krishna died at Dwaraka through an arow shot by Jara, the Savara. After the cremation it was found that the fire could not consume the heart of Sri Krishna, which was then thrown to the western sea at Dwarka. Jara, the Savara, became repentant when he came to know that his arrow had caused the death of the Lord. Repentant as he was, he started to follow the course of the holy heart, which ultimately reached the Puri coast. He collected the holy heart and installed it in the nearby forest for its daily *puja*. While floating on the seas, the heart *turned* into a blue stone. After Jara his descendants also became devotees of it. This blue stone was named "Nilamadhava". After a couple of centuries Indradyumna, king of Malava, desired to revive Vishnu *puja* in the country. But his problem was wherefrom he would get a pure and natural image of Vishnu. In a dream he saw the image of Nilamadhava. Soon after the sage Narada came to him and asked him to arrange for Vishnu puja, and for that purpose to take effective steps for searching the image of Nilamadhava. The king then sent emissaries to all sides of the country to find out the image. One of his Brahmin priests, Vidyapati by name, was entrusted to search the eastern side. During the course of his search Vidyapati reached a Savara village in the jungle of Odradesa on the sea coast and begged shelter of Vishwabasu, the Savara chief there, which was granted. While staying there the Brahmin noticed that the Savara chief had been going everyday, early morning all alone, to the jungles with *puja* offerings. He came to know from Lalita, the daughter of the Savara chief, that the purpose of the daily journey inside the jungles was for worshipping Nilamadhava, and this Nilamadhava was actually the holy heart of Lord Krishna, installed by their ancestors in the blue mountain inside the jungles. The young, good-looking Vidyapati fell in love with Lalita, in spite of the fact that he was a married man and his wife was living. He approached the Savara chief for the hands of Lalita. After persistent requests from the Brahmin and his daughter's approval to the proposal of marriage, the Savara chief accepted the Brahmin as his son-in-law On the very night of the marriage, Vidyapati got assurance from Lalita for visiting Nilamadhava.

Vidyapati then started insisting on the chief for taking him to Nilamadhava, a request to which the chief was not at all agreeable. The chief also told him that it was difficult to get Nilamadhava's audience, and it was particularly unbecoming for a foreigner to do so. Because of the persistent requests of the son-in-law and later of his daughter, the chief gave in and agreed to take him to Nilamadhava on condition that he would be blindfolded on his way and back. But as Vidyapati was very anxious to know the location of Nilamadhava, Lalita consoled her depressed husband by saying that some way out would be found. On the day of his visit to Nilamadhava, at the time of wrapping her husband's eyes with thick cloth, Lalita passed on to him some mustard seeds and advised him to sow these en route. The rainy season was near at hand, and these seeds would become saplings very soon and these will direct him to Nilamadhava. On reaching there one day after the rainy season the Savara chief found that on that day Nilamadhava did not accept his offerings. While the gloomy chief began praying to the deity for accepting his offerings he heard an oracle saying, "So long I have taken your offerings consisting of raw food and flowers. Now I desire to take cooked food fit to be offered to the king." Vidyapati's purpose was served, and so within a short period he took leave of his wife and hurriedly went back to Malava. There he narrated to the king his experience about Nilamadhava.

On hearing this King Indradyumna, accompanied by his soldiers, moved forward for Odradesa without much delay to seize Nilamadhava. On reaching the exact location, as directed by Vidyapati, he did not find any trace of the god. At that the king became angry, marched to the Savara village and arrested the Savara chief, Vishwabasu. Soon after this, the king

heard a celestial voice directing him, "Release the Savara, he is
my own man. Erect a temple on the blue mountain, and instal
me there in my new form as *darubrahma*." But wherefrom
would Nilamadhava in the form of *darubrahma* be available ?
In despair he decided to die, but soon after he heard another
divine commandment, "Early next morning I shall reach
Bankimuhan (near Chakratirth) on the sea coast floating as
darubrahma". Next morning the log was visible at the exact spot
and the king, failing to lift it, employed his soldiers and
elephants to haul it. But alas, all attempts of the king got
frustrated as the log could not be lifted. When the king was
full of dejection, he once more heard a celestial voice saying,
"Bring here my old attendant Vishwabasu, and request him and
Vidyapati to lift me from the sea." What a wonder!
Vishwabasu and Vidyapati could very easily lift the log and
placed it on the ground. Poet Sarala Dasa writes, "*Brahmana
ade tadai Savara ade uthai Sri Krishna ajnare se ucha
kanishtai*" (the log was held on one side by the Brahmin, and
on the other side by the Savara, and at the order of Sri Krishna
they easily lifted it).

The next step was the attempt to construct the image of
the Lord from the log. Indradyumna invited many expert
carpenters for the work, but they simply failed to make even a
mark on the log. At last, the divine architect, Vishwakarma,
reached there in the disguise of an aged carpenter, taking the
name of Ananta Maharana, and assured the king that he would
fashion the idol within twenty-one days provided he was left all
alone and the doors of the temple must remain closed all the
time he would be there inside. The king promised to abide by
the condition laid down by the aged carpenter. At that the
aged carpenter closed the doors of the temple and engaged
himself in completing the work. Meanwhile, Queen Gundicha
became worried when after fifteen days no sound from inside
was coming out, and she thought that possibly the aged carpenter
had expired. To console the queen, disregarding the advice of
his ministers and Vidyapati, the king opened the doors of the
temple. And lo, there was no trace of the carpenter inside the
temple; only three images were there, all incomplete and
deformed. The king became repentant at not having kept the
word of honour given to the carpenter, and feeling himself
guilty, decided to starve unto death. The emaciated king, in a
dream, was then told by Lord Jagannatha that, "In the Kali
Yuga I desire to have this form. Though my limbs and entire
body are not visible I shall accept *puja* and salutations from my

devotees." The king felt gratified on hearing the Lord's words. Lord Jagannatha then advised him, "to appoint the descendants of Jara Savara and of the Brahmin Vidyapati for carrying on daily rituals in the temple. The Savara chief Vishwabasu is my greatest devotee. His son should be known as my *pasupalaka* and his descendants as my *dayitas*. They would be my attendants. For one month every year I would be completely under their care; during that period I shall take service only from them and would take food from them only. The sons of Vidyapati's Brahmin wife would be my priests, and the sons of Vidyapati's Savara wife Lalita would be my cooks." Sarala Dasa writes, "*Vidyapati Brahmana je dutapane gala/Savara jhiyaku se je pradana hoila/Savarani thadu jeu heba jata/Suddha Suar se hetha bole Jagannatha/Savarara ghare jeu putra heba jata/dayita sevak heba bole Jagannatha.*

When the temple and the image were ready, the king, on the advice of the sage Narada, went to *Brahmaloka* for requesting Lord Brahma to consecrate the temple. Lord Brahma was then in deep meditation, for which the King Indradyumna had to wait there for nine *yugas* (one yuga of the god is 360 years of a human being). Meanwhile, the temple had sunk deep into the sands, and a new dynasty was ruling over there. One day when King Galamadhava of the new dynasty was passing by the beach, his horse suddenly stopped his movement. He found that one of legs of the horse was stuck to something inside the sand, and the horse was unable to make any movement with that leg. The king then started digging the sand, and found that the hoof of the horse was stuck on something very hard. When he could release the leg of the horse, he found that the hard object was a trident. He became curious and ordered his people to dig further on the spot. Ultimately, a temple was visible, but there was no idol inside it. While he was thinking of placing some idol inside the temple, King Indradyumna along with Lord Brahma arrived on the scene. When a dispute arose between Galamadhava and Indradyumna, Lord Brahma agreed to mediate. Witnesses came forward, the *bhusandi* crow (a mythical crow living through the ages), which had been living all the time on the 'wishing banyan tree' (*kalpa bat*) beside the temple, and also the turtles of the Indradyumna tank. It is said that these amphibians were originally human beings, but as a result of carrying heavy stones on their backs from the mountain at the time of erection of the Jagannatha temple under orders of the King Indradyumna, they had turned into turtles, and then they took shelter at the tank

which was named after Indradyumna (it may be mentioned here
that even now there are many turtles in the tank) It may also
be noted here that the tortoise is a totem of the Solar race.
As the evidence went in favour of Indradyumna, Lord Brahma
instructed the king to make arrangements for purification and
inauguration of the temple. In the story composed by Sarala
Dasa it has been said that because of his killing the Savaras,
Jagannatha cursed Galamadhava with childlessness.   In his words,
"*Madhava koile raja to mandya kritva kalu   Savara putranta
mora kimpai mailu / mama bhagatanku kalu jhingasa   Oh
Galavaraja tora na rahiba vamsha*   In the story of Bipra
Nilambara it is seen that King Indradyumna prayed to Jagannatha
for granting him his desire to be childless.   But why such a
peculiar prayer by Indradyumna ?   It says that the king desired
such a boon so that in his absence there would be no
impropriety in the matter of worshipping the god.

An analysis of the story will help in understanding how
fictitious it is.   Hindus take the story as fact and divine.   The
story centres round a king of Malava, Indradyumna by name.
No trace of such a king in Malava is available in history.   As
such this name was obviously an imagined one, and we can
take Indradyumna to be a mythical king.   Secondly, why did
the Brahmin Vidyapati, who was already married, became eager
to marry Lalita, the daughter of the Savara chief?   Was it
because this made it easier for him to plunder the idol of the
non-Aryan Savaras ?   Or, was the story an attempt to narrate the
fact of admixture of Aryan and non-Aryan blood ?   And why
so much eagerness for plundering a non-Aryan idol ?   In Sarala
Dasa's story we find the Brahmin's fervent begging for marrying
the Savara girl, whereas Bipra Nilambara narrates that the
Brahmin married the daughter of the Savara chief at the request
of the chief.   Bipra Nilambara's narration in many cases is just
the obverse of Sarala Dasa's ;   it should be noted that Sarala
Dasa's composition is older than that of Nilambara's, and that
whereas Sarala Dasa was a Sudra by caste, Nilambara was a
Brahmin. Nilambara's intention in obversing Sarala Dasa can be
surmised.   Moreover, it is Sarala Dasa's story that is more
popular among the people.

The Hindu pantheon of gods and goddesses is so large that
it is almost equal to the stars in the sky.   Then why such
attempts on the part of the Hindus to plunder the non-Aryan
Savara deity ?   To placate the Buddhists, Gautama Buddha was
accepted by the Hindus as one of their *avataras*, a clever step

that the Hindus took. In Orissa, the kings needed the help of the Savaras and other primitive races to maintain their kingdom. Then, there is the story of Nilamadhava, the Savara deity, which ultimately turned into a log of wood. It has already been narrated how the 'holy heart' of Sri Krishna, thrown on the western sea, could reach the eastern sea at Puri, where at first it took the shape of a blue stone, and later on became a log. The story raises many questions because of its irrelevancies. A few points about the absurdities of such myths may be discussed here. Firstly, when the 'holy heart' was thrown into the western sea, it should have floated down south to the Indian ocean. It was indeed a miracle that a human heart could manoeuvre itself to take a left about turn for entering the eastern sea and float upwards. Secondly, when the human heart reached Puri it turned into a blue stone, and when the king got it, it again turned into a log of wood, which was named *darubrahma*. Such metamorphoses can happen only in a fantasy Thirdly, the small piece of wood became so heavy that the king, even with the help of his army and elephants could not draw it upon the shore, whereas the Savara chief could lift it easily with the help of his Brahmin son-in-law. Then again, when the wood was taken overboard, a thousand axes could not cut it, because of which the engineer-deity, Vishwakarma, had to be invoked, and then it was cut easily. Miracle after miracle ! Moreover, why was there such an oracle, according to which the non-Aryan Savara chief and his descendants were allotted important offices in the matter of daily *puja* of the deity, and were named as *dayitas* of the Lord ? Why so much fuss and hullabaloo over depicting the Savara deity as Lord Vishnu /Sri Krishna? The attempts to prove that it was a Hindu deity, and that a Vaishnava one, do not naturally cut ice. It is clear from these stories that this deity was originally a Savara deity. There was no harm in declaring that this non-Aryan deity is being taken into the Hindu fold. But Hindus were and are at home in mytholising every thing. Then again, the story says that when King Galamadhava dug deep into the sands, he found a trident on the top of the temple. It indicates that originally the temple was a Shivashakti temple, not a Vaishnava one.

So, can we not reach the conclusion that the marriage of the Savara chief's daughter with the Brahmin emissary, acceptance of all the demands by the king himself— all these indicate that the Savaras were won over by the sharp and witty diplomacy of the Hindu kings ? And that is the main theme of the legends.

Strictly speaking, Hinduism is not a religion. It is a way of life. Many non-Aryan gods and goddesses have been elevated into Hindu deities. The process of assimilation of tribal gods and goddesses into the Hindu pantheon has gone on ever since the Aryans invaded Bharatavarsha. There is no better example of this process of assimilation than the elevation of the Savara godling into Lord Jagannatha. Since the aboriginal Savaras were animists, they could not conceive a human form for their deities. The incongruous Jagannatha is the best example of this process. The process is not yet complete.   That is why we have the ridiculous icons of Jagannatha and other deities in the Puri temple.

CHAPTER VII

THE SUN GOD

SUN IS a bright and luminous god. Its heat generates life, the organs of the body become conscious and active. He is supposed to be the creator, regulator and protector of the universe. In *Rg-Veda* it has been stated that the Sun is the container of boundless energy, he is like the *atman* of all mobile and immobile forces (*Apra dyabaprithvi chantarikshan Surya atma Jagatastasthusacha* - i/15/1). He traverses the world in a chariot driven by seven horses. The severe heat destroys the virus of diseases, and purifies the atmosphere. On one side he seems to be terrible, on the other he is compassionate. Since the dawn of creation, the Sun is the original source and sustainer of worldly life. He expels darkness, and destroys sins. *Samba Purana* says that the Sun is the creator and preserver, the origin and begetter of all living animals. It does not decay and it stays in an imperishable sphere (*Esha dhata bidhata cha bhutadir bhutabhabanah/na hyesa kshyamayati nityamkshaya mandalah* - 2/11). According to Yaska the three chief gods are Agni on the earth, Surya or Sun in the sky, and Vayu or Indra in the intervening region between the Sun and other planets.

Since ancient times the Sun has been recognised to be the chief god not only in India, but also in Egypt, Babylon and other countries. During the Vedic and post-Vedic age the Sun had an important place in the religious life of India. The Sun was worshipped in the form of a round red circle on stones. Sun worship is mentioned in *Ramayana, Mahabharata,* and in Puranas like *Agni, Vayu, Matsya, Markandeya, Padma, Samba, Skanda, Baraha, Bhavishya,* etc. as well as in the Buddhist scriptures. The *Satpatha Brahmana* states, "*Aditya ba etadbagra asit*" (1/7/4), which means that the Aditya (Sun) was born before others; it also states in verse no. 2/3/3 that the Sun is the begetter of all other gods. The *Samba Purana* in verse no. 2/19 says that the gods like Brahma, Vishnu, Shiva are only heard in legends, but the Sun is visible in destroying darkness and is our primordial god. In another verse (2/12) it states that the Sun is the father of all the fathers, god of all the gods. In the *Rg-Vedic* hymns reverence for the Sun abounds in the account of the functions and qualities of the Sun. In the *Aranyakas, Upanisads,* and *Grihyasutras* the Sun has been recognised as identical with Lord Brahma. Hymns adoring the Sun are also found in the *Tantras*. The *Ramayana* states that Agastya Muni advised Sri Ramachandra to worship the Sun for killing Ravana. In various chapters of the *Mahabharata* like Adi, Vana, Anushasana, Udyog, and Karna, worshipping of the Sun is mentioned. Even the details for worshipping the Sun god are given in the Vana Parva. It is from the *Mahabharata* we come to know that to control the severe heat of the Sun, Vishwakarma cut down one-eighth part from the body of the Sun, and from the choppped portion of its body Vishwakarma manufactured the wheel for Vishnu and the trident for Shiva. In *Markandeya Purana* the place of the Sun has been given above the Hindu Trinity, Brahma-Vishnu-Maheshwara.

In the first part of the post-Gupta age a member of Harsavardhan's assembly, Mayura, composed the *Surya Sataka*. He was a leprosy patient, and after recovering from the disease he composed these poems adoring the Sun. From archaeological findings it is known that during the Saka-Kusana rule Mathura and nearby places were important centres of Sun worship. A large number of idols of the Sun have been recovered from this area. From different stone inscriptions it has been gathered that during the pre-and-post Gupta age many Sun temples were erected at various places. From the Mundasor stone inscription of Kumaragupta the First, it is known that in the fifth century a vast and beautiful Sun temple was erected. Burgess states in his book that a large number of Sun temples have been found in the area between Multan and Kutch. Mentioning various inscriptions, Sankalia has said that Sun worship was widespread in the entire Gujarat area. The Martanda temple to the Sun in Kashmir was built in the eighth century. Tanjore in South India also had a Sun temple.

The Ananta Cave in Orissa is a witness to the prevalence of Sun worship there. The cave is of the 2nd century B.C. While digging it, an idol of the Sun, sitting on his chariot, was found. In several stories in Oriya language it has been stated that Samba, son of Sri Krishna, came to Konark on the bank of the river Chandrabhaga for the purpose of worshipping the Sun god, and that Samba built a stone idol of the Sun there. Konark is, of course, known as humming with adoration to the Sun god. In the ninth century Puranda Kesari of the Soma dynasty erected a Sun temple there. Today Konark is attracting visitors from all over the world for its Sun temple. This temple was built by the King Narasimha Deva of the Ganga dynasty. Carvings of the Sun sitting on the chariot and driven by four horses are engraved at Varahanath temple on the bank of the river Vaitarini at Jajpur, and at the Lingaraja temple of Bhubaneswar. In the precincts of the Jagnnatha temple complex there is a Sun temple, and the *Aruna Stambha* (pillar of the Sun) has been placed at the entrance of the temple. This was, of course, brought down from Konark and placed here. There was a custom in the Pauranic age to worship nine planets along with the Sun. In most of the temples in Orissa nine planets are kept along with other deities. We are quoting here the story as found in the *Samba Purana*. It runs thus :

Samba was the son of Sri Krishna. He was accused by Sri Krishna of being smitten with carnal desire for the wives of Sri Krishna and leading the ladies astray, for which he was cursed by the Lord with leprosy. Samba thus became a leper. On the advice of the sage Narada, the leper Samba left Dwarka for the Arkakshetra (Sun's place) in North India, reaching where he, with earnest mind, began to worship the Sun god. He invoked the Sun constantly for curing him from the disease. The Sun ultimately blessed him after twelve years of penance. After becoming cured of the disease, while he was taking bath in the river Chandrabhaga, he found an idol of the Sun inside the water. He installed the idol there. This Arkakshetra is Multan (now in Pakistan) in the Punjab on the bank of the river Chandrabhaga.

Even during the Mughal days the emperor Akbar introduced Sun worship. His directive was to worship the Sun daily in the morning, afternoon, evening, and at mid-night. He collected 1001 names of the Sun from the Sanskrit literatures, and facing the Sun, he used to recite those names. At that time he used to hold his ears, and afterwards patted the place in between his head and neck. His son Jehangir also was a worshipper of the Sun. W. Crooke in his book *Things Indian* has mentioned these facts.

From the Pauranic days Vishnu started gaining the exalted position accorded to the Sun. It is said that the Sun spread himself out in twelve forms, and Vishnu is his ninth form. As Vishnu he appeared on the scene to kill demons. Possibly because of this displacement no new Sun temple came up after the one at Konark. The Sun has now become Surya-Narayana. Of course, it is true that though no temples are coming up, the place of the Sun in the heart of the Indians is constant. Hindus worship the Sun every moring with the sacred *Gayatri mantra*(hymns), *"Om, bhurbhubcsya tatsavitar barenyam Bharga devasya dhimati dhiyona pracholayat"* (Let us mediate on the splendid effulgence of Savitar. concentrated mind of the gods, may he enlighten our minds).

Now, who are the guards of this Sun god? *Samba Purana* says, *"Rakshastyudyata-shastrastra Yaksha-Rakshasa-Pannagah"* (6/15), which means that Yakshas, Rakshasas and Nagas guard the Sun, ever alert, with weapons. *Puranas* say that in different ages, gods, and specially Vishnu, appeared to annihilate these Yakshas; Rakshasas and the Nagas. From this fact again, we can conclude that these non-Aryans were devotees of the Sun. To the primitives of India, the Sun god is the supreme one ; this conception has been recognised by the Hindu Puranas.

Encyclopaedia of Religion and Ethics states that there is a close relation between the Sun and the *neem* tree. In the ancient days Solar worshippers were in abundance and they were also influential. As Shaktas have 51 holy places, Vaishnavites have 12, Solar worshippers had 7 such holy places, and these were well spread out in different parts of the country. Multan, Konark and such places were marked as *Suryakshetra* (place of the Sun). To the Solar worshippers the *neem* tree was very sacred. W Crooke in his book *The Popular Religion and Folklore of Northern India* states that in a specially modified form a group of Vaishnavites worship the Sun. They are known as Nimbarkas (Nimba, i.e. *neem* and Arka, i.e. Sun). It should be noted here that as there is a relation between leprosy and the Sun (Sun is supposed to cure leprosy), so there is a relation between the Sun and the *neem* tree. It is also generally known that the juice of the *neem* helps curing leprosy and skin diseases.

Another Death Before Death

Leprosy is a dreadful disease. In most of the ancient literatures of the world as in the *Talmud*, in the *Bible*, and in Egypt, in Latin, and in India, this disease has been described with fear, dread and repulsion for the sufferers. The Egyptians thought that this was an incurable disease, and they used to say that it was a death before the physical death. In the *Bible* and in the *Talmud* this disease has been referred to a number of times. From the *Bible* we come to know that bricks were thrown when a leper was in sight. Being the fatalists that the Hindus are, they thought that this disease was due to sins committed in ast lives. Herodotus wrote that the Persians held this disease to be due to the curse of the Sun. In *Things Indian*, W. Crooke has written that many believe that a person who kills another by treachery gets this disease. He has mentioned certain cases. These are: treacherous Samil killed the emperor Feroze Shah and within two years Samil became inflicted with this disease; that a Portuguese Friar thought that those who killed St. Thomas, the messenger of god, they and their descendants suffered from this disease; that the Thugs used to think that if any one of them commits treason by killing one amongst themselves, he will suffer from this disease; that some people think that this is caused because of Sati's curse. However, the majority believe that this disease is caused due to the curse of the angry Sun god. There are many remedial prescriptions, one being to live for twelve years uncovered under a *neem* tree. The *Atharva Veda* prescribes *castus speciosus* for this disease. In the *Kaushitaki Brahmana* the sufferers have been directed to worship the Maruts. The *Atharva Veda* has also advised the adoration of the Maruts.

We find that the *neem* leaves have a connection with the cure of leprosy. In the *Dhanwantari Nighantu* and in *Shaligram Nighantubhusanam* the juice of *neem* leaves have been prescribed. Dr C.R. Mitra, in his book NIM, says that the *neem* is an accompanying concomitant of chaulmugra in treatment of leprosy. He has also referred to a prevalent notion amongst us that the ghosts who accompany the dead body do not want to come in touch with the leaves of *neem*, as these leaves are supposed to help in chasing the ghosts away. Though it was a belief current among the primitives, such beliefs are also noticed among the caste Hindus. It is a custom among the Hindus that before entering the house after cremation, one is to take a *neem* leaf in the mouth.

In India we have known of this disease since 1400 B.C. It is but natural that it has been dreaded since that time. It is a pitiful sight to find a healthy and strong person becoming mutilated, when attacked with this disease. Very naturally people are frightened of this disease. From an investigation published in *India Today* (31.10.82) it is known that in India there are more than 32 lakhs (3 million plus) leper patients, and that 40 lakhs (4 million) more have possibility of getting it. In the world there are more than one crore (10 million) leprosy patients. It has been noticed that this disease is more prevalent among the tribal population in India and, in fact, 80% of the leprosy patients in India are aboriginals. A report placed in the Andhra Pradesh

Legislative Assembly in 1982 states that the number of leprosy patients there is 6 lakhs and 3 thousand, the majority of whom belong to the primitive tribes. In a Press Conference held at Bhunbaneswar in August 1982, Nityananda Mishra, M.P. from Bolangir, told a harrowing tale. He said that 20% of the population of Bolangir and 80 to 90% population of the Bolangir sub-division are leprosy patients. The Adibasi and Harijan Research and Training Centre of Bhubaneswar investigated the matter, and they have found that out of the population of Orissa the primitive tribal population is 40% and 70% of them are lepers.

From the facts mentioned above it can be assumed that the prevalence of leprosy among the primitives in Orissa is a long standing scourge. Similarly, the belief that the Sun's heat helps in curing this disease has also been prevalent since early times. It has been prescribed that for getting cured of this disease, it is advisable to drink in the rays of the rising sun, the mid-day sun, and the setting sun. To the Savaras, the relatives of Jagannatha, the Sun or Uyungsun is the supreme god. They believe that if the god gets angry he will inflict them with leprosy. They also know that this Sun god also helps to cure leprosy. They adore not one but many gods, only to get rid of this disease. Apart from Uyungsen, the other gods are Darammasun, Kumbirsum, Madusum, Muttasing, and a few others. The wild tribes residing in the mountains of Orissa and Madhya Pradesh are also devotees of the Sun. When danger looms large, Kharwars worship the Sun ; Bhuiyas and Oraons adore the Sun god as Dharma devata or Boram; Kharias worship the Sun as Bero. The villagers of the plains worship the Sun in the name of Surya-Narayana. It has already been mentioned that this area was and still now is heavily affected with leprosy.

That this disease was widespread in Orissa can be gauged from local folklores. Verrier Elwin is his book *Tribal Myths of Orissa* has published many folklores. It is apparent that as the Sun god is recognised to be the god who cures leprosy, in whatever name it is called, it has become the supreme god to those aboriginals.

CHAPTER VIII

JAGANNATHA CULTURE : ORIGIN AND DEVELOPMENT

VARIOUS MYTHS and legends have been circulated to convince people of the antiquity of Lord Jagannatha. Some have sought its origin in pre-*Mahabharata* times. Whatever that might be, the matter needs to be debated judiciously. But it is perfectly true that centring on this uncouth and grotesque image a unique religious culture has evolved. Many religious beliefs originated after the Aryan invasion of India, and the old literatures have depicted many stories about conflicts and confrontations between various religious groups. Not only in ancient literature, these have been recorded in many works of the historical age also. Of course, the stories of such conflicts have not been recorded in the ancient literature in a straightforward way ; these have been expressed through stories of the supernatural and magic. Religionists were careful in hiding true facts, and to keep such conflicts amongst themselves hidden from the public eye, these religio-propagandists concocted queer stories. Since the Aryan invasion till recent times such conflicts, leading to murder and bloodshed, were in abundance. In this connection, Khushwant Singh writes in his column in *Sunday,* dated 13-19 April, 1986 that, "D.N. Roy and Indira Devi in their book *Kumbha : India's Ageless Festival* (1958) gave an unflattering account of what happened at these festivals. Crowds assembled in their milllions. There were factional fights resulting in heavy toll of life. Less known of many ghastly tragedies was a pitched battle fought between Gosains and Bairagis at Hardwar in 1780 A.D. in which 18,000 men were killed. In another fracas at the same place in 1795, Sikh pilgrims slew 500 Gosains." However, such conflicts were more or less firstly between Aryans and non-Aryans, then between the Buddhists and the Brahmins, between Shaiva-Shakta and the Vaishnavites. Internecine conflicts between sub-sects of those religious groups are also on record. These religionists were engaged in such unnecessary conflicts and bloodshed, solely with the object of attaining supremacy.

Brahminism had to take recourse to compromising with the non-Aryans for the sake of expediency. Otherwise it would not have survived against the strong thrust made by the Buddhists. As a result of this compromise, they were obliged to accommodate the beliefs of the Dravidians and the primitives. What came out is Popular Hinduism, in which very little of

Aryan belief have survived. After overcoming the onslaught of Buddhism, the Hindus created among themselves many different religious sects, and started struggling among themselves for taking the supreme position. Disgraceful is the Hindu religious history because of its infighting and killing among various Hindu sects and groups. And why Hinduism only, all the religions of the world bear the same history. True that with the progress of civilisation, such open conflicts among the different Hindu religious communities are waning away for political reasons, but even now their impotent forms are noticeable. They have lost absolute political power, but what about their influence in society? It is very much still there, though in a subdued form.

In this situation, Orissa's religious history is something different, actually it is unique. Here all the religious off-shoots of Hinduism got royal patronage, and cases of violent conflicts are rare. In fact, a possibility arose of shaping completely a new religious form around the deity, Jagannatha. It is not a cult, as many scholars say, it is a new religious culture that grew around this deity. It is a synthesis emerging out of different religious faiths—non-Aryans and different Hindu and non-Hindu faiths. An unrefined and deformed god of the wild primitive Savaras gave birth to such an unpararelled religious culture, where all other religious beliefs got submerged. And because of such an outcome, all Indian religious communities claim the fatherhood of this diety. Such a synthesis is rare in Indian religious history, where there is a plethora of gods and goddesses. All the religious communities, whether they are Jainas, Buddhists, Shaivites, Saktas, Ganapatyas, Vaishnavites or Solar worshippers, all illustrate this deity in their own language. This Jagannatha has absorbed into itself all these beliefs. This synthesis is apparent in the daily hymns meant for this deity. In the hymns the deity is being worshipped as a representative of different religious groups. The hymn runs thus : *Jang Darubrahma Murtim Pranabatanudharam/ sarvavedanta saram/ Bhaktanam Kalpabriksha Bhabajalataranee/ Sarvatakhanukham Yoginam Hansattwam Harihara namita/ Sreepati Vaishnavanam/ Shaibanam Bhairavasyam Pashupati paramam / Shaktatattwe Shaibatam cha / Bauddhanam Bauddhasapat Rupa bhayati baro/ Jainasiddhantamurtih / Tam Deva patu Nityam Kali Kalusaharam O Nilashiladhinatha.*

Local environment begets local needs, which again produce a culture befitting the environment. All through the ages, since time immemorial, man has known that there is something which is much more powerful than he. From this inherent idea men started adoring so many things like wild animals, trees, rivers, mountains, etc. At that early age they did not imagine the modelling of an anthropomorphic image. The anthropomorphic image of man as god is a more recent innovation. In spite of this conception, not only in India, but also among the aboriginals of the underdeveloped world, that early belief, i.e.worshipping trees, etc., still prevails. Every Hindu image has its own mount —it might be a mouse, goose, tiger, or elephant. Another name of Shiva is *Pashupati* (lord of the animals) In fact, these are nothing but reflections of non-Aryan beliefs. It may be that now-a-days wild animals are not being worshipped by the primitives, but they call themselves after different animals, which are their totems. The tree, however, is still being adored by them, whether in its full form or as a piece of log. Actually, the trees or its leaves had been an essential element of worship since early days. Even in the Hindu society worshipping of banyan, pipul, marmaloes, etc. is still in currency. This idea of worshipping a tree has come from the primitives. According to Hindu customs the marmeloes tree is associated with Shiva, basil is related to Narayana, *neem* with Shitala. Besides, leaves and twigs of pipul, banyan, mango, marmaloes, fig, etc. and even grass (*durba*) are used for different Hindu *pujas*. A section of Shaivites in Karnataka respect *neem* tree as Shiva's genital. Though worshipping tree has been abandoned in the western countries, echoes of this speciality survive in the Christmas tree, May pole, etc. And it has been earlier mentioned that the aborigines, particularly those who reside around the Vindhyas, do not model any anthropomorphic image of their gods—they worship a tree, or a log. And we find that Jagannatha is held to be *darubrahma*.

In spite of the fact that the Hindus treated their wooden deity as *darubrahma*, the question arises whether the Savaras knowingly agreed to give their consent to such transformation of their deity. It has been understood that they initially did not do so with open hearts. They thought that the Brahmins plundered their god. A folklore in this connection has been narrated on pages 31-32. Another story is also being narrated here

An aged Savara of the village Seori-Narayana in the Bilaspur district (South Kosala) used to worship a wooden deity, representing the Sun god. The wooden deity was so well-known and respected all around that the king of Puri came to know of it. At that time the king was erecting a massive temple at Puri. He thought of installing the wooden idol of Seori-Narayana at this temple, and for that purpose sent a Brahmim emissary to Seori-Narayana. But nobody knew of the exact location of the idol, except the aged Savara. The Brahmin wanted to see the idol. But all the solicitations of the Brahmin fell on deaf ears of the Savara. Ultimately, the Brahmin offered himself for marriage with the daughter of the Savara. After the marriage, at the persisent solicitations of the Brahmin son-in-law, the Savara gave his consent, but he told him that he will have to be blindfolded on the way to the god and back. On the day of visiting the idol the Savara wife of the Brahmin gave him some mustard seeds and advised him to strew the seeds on the way to the idol. After some time, when the mustard saplings were visible, the Brahmin went into the forest all alone to seek the idol's location. Arriving there he begged the deity for travel along with him to Puri, where the king was waiting for him to which the idol Surya-Narayana at last agreed. The deity told him that he would not travel with him, he will reach Puri as a log of wood floating over the river Mahanadi. Soon after, the old Savara came to know of it and started weeping before the deity, at which the god told him that he desired to be offered delicious cooked food, and he had no more desire to take raw and uncooked food. To console the Savara, the god told him that from then on the place will be named after the name of the idol, combined with the Savara's. Since then the place is known as Seori-Narayana (Seori, i.e.Savara, and Narayana of Surya-Narayana).

This story is narrated in detail in the *Bilaspur Gazette, 4th volume,* p. 800.

If we compare this Savara legend and the other one mentioned in pages 31-32 with that of the Indradyumna one, a very close similarity between them will be found. From these and other stories, it appears that the present Jagannatha image came to Puri from South Kosala, i.e. Western Orissa. Hislop comments in the *Census of India, Vol. IV, Part I,* 1911 that at the sight of the image of Jagannatha he felt that this idol came down to Puri from the mountains of the Ganjam district and that there was a· peculiar similarity of this idol with the deformed Kittung images of that district.

In the later part of the 13th century the wild Saoras attacked the temple, which was resisted successfully by the priests under the leadership of the Vaishnava guru Narahari Tirth. This matter has been reported in *South Indian Inscriptions,* which also states that this incident could be known from the only inscription in the Kurmeshwara temple at Srikarman, which area is full of wild Saoras. G.V. Sitapati has also referred to a rebellion of the Saoras in his article in the *Journal of Andhra Historical Research Society, Vol.XII.* Besides, the *Sambalpur Gazetter, 1st part, 1979,* has mentioned that in 1981 there was an attempt to plunder the image from inside the temple and to burn it. From the *Jagannatha Temple Correspondence, No. 224,* it is understood that a team of barbarians consisting of 12 males and 3 females attacked the temple for burning the images of Jagannatha-Balabhadra-Subhadra, and they could be halted only after they had reached the *bhogamandap* of the temple. It is also known that they brought with them a pot of cooked rice and wanted to eat inside the temple for making the deities impure. The attackers belonged to the Kumbhipatia sect (people wearing barks of the Kumbhi tree Kumbhi is yellow cotton) and their intention was to convince others about the untrue nature of the Jagannatha worship as it was being carried on This religious community does not have any faith in discrimination on the basis of caste and class. It is apparent that they wanted to protest against the introduction of caste discrimination in the temple. The Court verdict went against the tribals. It said that these uncivilised people of low caste, who do not have any respect for the age-old caste system, have no right to enter the Jagannatha temple. This community is also known as the followers of the Mahima Dharma. They are mostly low caste Hindus and tribals. From these incidents it can be assumed that they rose in rebellion in support of their age-old belief about the Jagannatha idol, which belief was then being systematically demolished by the Hindus. They had grounds for such rebellion, as even when the deity was recognised to have been originally a Savara deity, they are now debarred from entering even the first gate of the temple under the influence of Brahminism. It is understood that the untouchables and the low caste people were prohibited from entering the temple in the first part of the 18th century. It should also be noted here that the team of the Kumbiipatias came from the mountainous area of the district of Sambalpur. And this district is thickly populated by the aborigines. Though no document giving any reason for such attacks on the image by the aborigines is produced, would it be wrong if it is assumed that these incidents are the end-results of the plundering and reconstructing of the image of their deity, and of demolishing all their customs and beliefs?

From all reports it is found that indications of such rebellion started during the days of the Ganga dynasty, and some such incidents continued till the 19th century— revolts not only by the outsiders, but also by the priests. If the time span of such incidents is considered, it could be noticed that rebellion started when the temple was going under the control of the Vaishnavites, and during the period of their absolute control Strange it is, as the Vaishnavites themselves do not believe in any form of class and caste distinction. It can be called degradation of their cult. Close on the heels of such incidents suspicion arises about the antiquity of the idol, and about the name of Jagannatha as well in the Hindu pantheon. Dr H.K.Mahtab says in his book (*History of Orissa*) that the name of Jagannatha first appeared in the 18th century A.D. in the book "Jagannatha" written by Indrabhuti. Dr D.C.Sarkar in an article in the *Journal of Asiatic Society of Bengal, Vol. No.17*, has written that first mention of Jagannatha has been found in the Srikuram temple inscription of 1309 and in the Simhachalam inscription of 1319 of the king Bhanudeva the Second. Even if the antiquity of the deity be not repudiated, it can be concluded that the naming of this deity as Jagannatha is comparatively modern. It can be presumed that introducing the idol as Jagannatha was done during the 13th-14th centuries, after which the revolts started. Though Indrabhuti, king of Sambal, mentioned the name Jagannatha, there is no clear evidence that by that name he referred to the idol of the Puri temple. It should be noted here that Indrabhuti was a Buddhist, and a Vajrayani one. Hence, the claim of Indrabhuti can be discounted. It seems that the name Jagannatha of the Puri temple was preceded by names like Purushottama, Nrisimha, Patitapavana, and Dadhivamana as one goes back in time. It should be considered when the transformation of the original idol into its present form was made, when the three idols were placed along with Jagannatha, and whether, amongst the four, the Jagannatha image is the oldest. In this connection it should be remembered that not once but several times the image had to be transferred to other places from Puri, and that after the image was burnt down it had to be made again. Also the legends about these images need to be examined.

Apart from the attacks on the image of Jagannatha by the wild Savaras, quite a few such attempts have been by the heretics. *Madala Panji* states that Yayati Kesari Mahashivagupta recovered this image in a very much fragmented condition from the Sonepur-Baudh area of Orissa. It states that during the time of invasion of Orissa by Raktabahu, the heretic, the image was taken away from Puri and kept hidden. After 144 years the king

Yayati Kesari engaged himself in searching the "Lord of Orissa" (*Odisa Rajara Prabhu*), and succeeded in recovering it in fascicule condition (*Sedine Se Murtimane mati khai chhinna bhinna haichhanti*). It is to be noted here that the broken parts of the idol was recovered from Yayati Kesari's home area. In an earlier chapter it has been mentioned that those Kesari kings of the Soma dynasty were actually scions of the Savaras. Since early times wooden deities were worshipped under royal patronage in the Sonepur-Baudh area. According to *Madala Panji*, during the aggression of Raktabahu (there was no such king with this name; scholars think that it was an aggression by the Rashtrakutas of the South), the Brahmin priests and the Savara *dayitas* fled from Puri along with the image. And along with the fragmented parts of the idol, King Yayati Kesari brought the descendants of the Brahmin priests and the Savara *dayitas* to Puri from that area, and handed over to them the responsibility of modelling the image and worshipping it. In other words, the Savaras were brought down to Puri for the above-mentioned purposes from South Kosala, where the worship of crude wooden image was widespread. The question here naturally arises — when the wooden figure remained immersed under the earth for 144 years, and when it was recovered in a broken state of disfigurement, how could it be recognised as the figure of Jagannatha? And if that image was brought to Puri centuries before the Yayati era, should we assume that at that time Brahmin priests and Savara *dayitas* were engaged in that temple? Yayati Kesari proclaimed himself a Kshatriya, then why he, instead of installing a Hindu deity, brought in from afar the wooden deity of the Savaras and invested those wild peoples with the responsibility of modelling the image and of sharing the ritual technicalities of *puja* with the Brahmin priests?

There are many resemblances in the legends about the deity Jagannatha with Yayati Kesari's story. Let us consider some of these. Firstly, King Indradyumna sent emissaries to different places in search of the Nilamadhava. Yayati Kesari also engaged himself in searching for the "Lord of Orissa" (not Lord of the world, i.e. Jagannatha), and both of them Indradyumna and Yayati Kesari engaged forces for the purpose. Secondly, Indradyumna could secure the *darubrahma* on the sea coast of Puri, whereas Yayati Kesari could get it in a decayed condition beneath a tree in his home province. Thirdly, both of them modelled the image in wood, built temples, and for the purpose of modelling and worshipping the deity appointed Brahmin priests and the Savara *dayitas*. History does not recognise any Malava king named as Indradyumna, but Yayati Kesari is there in the records. In later days, after about 20 years from the burning of the image by Kalapahada, a part was recovered and Ramachandra Deva, the then king of Khurdah, installed a new image, for which Madala Panji calls him Indradyumna the Second. Moreover, *Madala Panji* and other books speak of only one image; Yayati Kesari also speaks of only *"Odisha Deshera Prabhu"*.

As regards the *Madala Panji* there is no definite record about its time of composition. There are more or less three opinions among the scholars. Dr H.K. Mahtab and some others think that it was composed during the Ganga dynasty's rule. The second opinion is that it was composed during the rule of the Surya dynasty. Dr Prabhat Mukherjee, Dr K.C. Panigrahi and others determine it to have been composed during the rule of the Khurdah rajas. In any case, none of the scholars think that it was composed before the Ganga rule. In the religious history of Orissa, and particularly that of Jagannatha, major changes started occurring from the Ganga rule. To legitimise their rule and their beliefs, as the kings came from outside, they felt the necessity of manufacturing myths. However, it can be concluded that the mythical Indradyumna was none other than Yayati Kesari. Apart from the resemblances mentioned above, it is to be noticed that in these myths no word has been uttered about the trinity or four-fold images, only one image has been dealt with. In fact, in no pre-Ganga inscription mention has been made of the trinity. Moreover, in the inscriptions during the Soma dynasty's rule neither Nrisimha, nor Purushottama nor Jagannatha has been mentioned. It should also be remembered here that the image had to be shifted from Puri on several occasions. Kalapahada got hold of the image in an island of the Chilika Lakes in 1568 and he burnt it there. During the later part of the 16th century King Ramachandra Deva built the new image and arranged for its *Nava Kalebara* (new body). Later, during the period between 1590 and 1750, the images had to be shifted to other places twelve times as precaution against continuous Muslim invasions. It has been earlier narrated that one Bisar Mohanty got the *brahmamani* of the Lord from the Chilika coast and took it to his village, where he started worshipping it. When King Ramachandra Deva got this information, he arranged to bring it to Puri in 1586. It is a popular and widely prevalent notion (belief) that if anybody sees or touches the *brahmamani,* he will not only be treated as a sinner but that he, for this act, will also face death soon after. But the story about Bisar Mohanty says that he not only saw and touched it, he brought it to his village and worshipped it for more than fifteen years. So, ·in spite of committing the sin of seeing and touching the *brahmamani,* Bisar did not face an instant death. On the other hand, he was in perfect health. A case of mythical disinformation! Another point that comes in along with it is when nobody could see it with his own eyes, how could Bisar recognise it as the Lord's *brahmamani* ?

Though the image of Jagannatha is not modelled on a human form, in its daily *puja* the rituals relate to the customs and habits of a human being, in fact the habits of a king. The daily rites have been narrated in earlier pages. These rites are followed meticulously. From the early dawn the temple hums with activities till mid-night. Really, a sumptuous and grandiose arrangement for the god. In the daily rites, besides the Brahmin priests, Savara *dayitas* have significant roles. They offer the deity breakfast in the morning, and on them remain the responsibility of cooking the *mahaprasada.* Besides, during the *Snan Yatra* (Bathing festival) and during *nava kalebara* they touch the body of the images, during the *jwaralila* (the deity gets fever after the *snan yatra*) they offer the deity medicinal decoction (actually sweet syrup), during the *Ratha Yatra* festival they carry the deities upto the main gate before placing them on the chariots, and during *anabasara* period (the days between *snan yatra* and *ratha yatra,* when the doors of the temple remain closed) they remain solely responsible for looking after the daily rites of the deities.

The role of the Savaras in performing varied rites in the Jagannatha temple has been detailed. Now-a-days, particularly after the almost absolute dominance of the Vaishnavites in the temple, the role of the Savaras has been and are being curtailed. Considering all the facts, it can be said that since the assimilation process of the temple activities started by the Hindus, the attempt to curb the role of the Savaras started, and that it has been a continuing process. Now they have more or less four responsibilities—cooking the food of the deities, looking after the deities during the *anabasara* period, during the *snan yatra* and *ratha yatra,* and during *nava kalevara.* After the *snan yatra* the gods become sick, and they have to be sick. Because, though *mantras* (hymns) are chanted in the Hindu style, the methods adopted are according to the Savara customs. According to the Hindus, bathing water should be clean river water, and turbid water in no case should be used for ceremonial ablutions. But the water that is used in the ablution for Jagannatha and other deities during *snan yatra* comes from a nearby completely shaded well called *swarna kupa*, i.e. golden well. According to the Savara belief, the water that is not kissed by the Sun's rays and situated in dense forest, is the best and most holy for worshipping a deity. To follow the Savara belief, the custom of bringing water for the ablution of the deities from the *swarna kupa*, situated at the northern end of the temple complex, is still in vogue. The water of the well does not come in touch with the rays of the sun, and it is very much turbid. The Lord is bathed with 108 pitchers of this turbid water. As it is the Lord, it survives ; it is almost impossible for a human being to survive if he is bathed with so much of turbid and filthy water. But the Lord falls sick for fifteen days, when the gates of the temple remain closed for outsiders. This is the *anabasara* period when there is no respite in offering homage to the deities, and all responsibilities of the deities are vested on the Savara *dayitas*. Brahmins have no right in offering worship to the deities during this time. The *dayitas* sit along with the deities on the platform, offer the deities fruits and roots, and they also partake in such feasts. After tasting sweet fruits they offer these to the deities, which even the Brahmin priests will not dare to do and are not authorised to do. The Savaras can offer such left-overs to the deities as they are the nearest relatives of the god. Moreover, as parents play with their children, they also do so with the deities in the same fashion. This peculiar form of devotion to the god seems to be undignified and barbarous to the Hindus, but that is the custom of these aboriginals. And such things inside the main temple goes on for fifteen days, when none is allowed to see it. To mytholise it the Hindus call it *gupta puja* (hindden worship).

The affinity and closeness of the Savaras with the deities and their role in the daily rites have been mentioned in brief. Now let us look at their role during the *nava kalevara* festivities. There is no fixed time for this ceremony, it may take ten to nineteen years time. Death of Jagannatha and his re-birth, that is what *nava kalevara* is. Preparation for this starts, when it is held, from the tenth day of the bright fortnight in the preceding Chaitra month (March-April). The wood from which the image is to be modelled is also washed during the *snanyatra* day. Particular *neem* trees, which have some special marks, are sought out, and from the wood of those trees the new images are modelled. For the four deities distinctive marks are set out. Four deities, i.e. Jagannatha, Balabhadra, Subhadra and Sri Sudarshana. It should be noted that along with the main three figures, Sri Sudarshana gets puja, and its *nava kalevara* has also to be done along with those of the other deities. Sudarshana is no figure, it is just a log kept colourfully dressed beside the Lord. There is a myth about this figure, which runs thus :

When Rohini, mother of Lord Krishna, was narrating in a closed room to the wives of Sri Krishna the stories of Shrimati Radha's courting episode, behind their eyes, outside the room, were Krishna, Balarama, Subhadra and Krishna's Sudarshana, who were attentively overhearing Rohini's narrations. While hearing the tales, they were afflicated with Cupid's arrow. And they were so afflicted that the limbs of Krishna and Balarama started contracting, eyes got enlarged, and Subhadra's limbs caved into her body; and the round wheel (Sudarshana) of Krishna melted in love and its round shape became stretched in length.

This is the myth, and it corresponds with the images that we find now in the Jagannatha temple. The absurdity of such a story needs no discussion. After all, fanciful imagination is the ground where religion treads.

From the day of going to the forest for collecting wood for *nava kalevara* till *rathayatra* and *punaryatra* (return journey) day, in almost all activities the Savaras have the priority. A team of about fifty people starts from the temple on the seventh day of the new moon for collecting wood. The team consists of 23 *dayitapatis* (chiefs of the *dayitas*) and *Pati Mahapatra* (descendants of Vidyapati's Brahmin wife—see legend), one Lenka, who carries the Sudarshana, 4 Vishwakarmas (carpenters), 3 accountants, 5 Brahmins for performing *yajnas* (vedic rites), a few sepoys and other attendants. Before the team starts the journey, *Pati Mahapatra,* after worshipping the deities, unfasten the four specially made garlands *(ajna mala)* from the deities, and hand over the three garlands prepared for Jagannatha- Balabhadra- Subhadra to the appointed *dayitapatis* (descendants of Vidyapati from his Savara wife). The garland for Sri Sudarshana is kept with the *Pati Mahapatra.* The garland for Balabhadra is called 'Bada-Bada', that of Subhadra 'Majhi-Bada', and of Jagannatha 'Mahaprabhunka-Bada' Before coming out of the temple, they get smeared with sandal paste and vermillion on their brows. Now along with the drum beats they will head to the king's palace, where the king will hand over to the Rajguru (royal priest) two salvers full of a few coconuts, few pieces of gold, few coloured holy threads and some unbroken rice. The Rajguru then passes over one salver to the Pati Mahapatra, and keeps the other one with him as the representative of the Brahmins. For final preparation of the journey thereafter the team takes shelter at the Jagannatha-Ballava *matha* (monastery) for a couple of days. Before they take up the journey *dayitapatis* worship goddess Bashuli (non-Aryan Shakti goddess) of Puri and pray to her for mercy. On the day of the journey they start at dawn for Kakotpur on the side of the river Prachi, 34 miles off Puri. They are to stop there for worshipping Mangala Devi (a form of Shakti). Near this place there is a thick forest of neem trees The priests of Mangala Devi go forward along with beating of the percussion drums to welcome the team, and to take them to the temple of the goddess. Only the Brahmins and the Pati Mahapatra stay in the temple complex as here the goddess will direct the Pati Mahapatra through dream to the location of the neem trees with special marks. To get this divine direction, the team stays there for a couple of days and worship the goddess daily, praying for her commandments. *Durgasaptasati* (hymns to Durga) is read out during the pujas of the goddess. If there be no oracle during three days, arrangements for special *puja* of the goddess are to be made with heaps of flowers. It is said that flowers will fall from the hands of this idol to indicate the direction, after which the team goes into the forest. From Kakotpur the team divides itself in four groups for searching the wood for the four deities. The principal dayitapati of each group is called *baragrahi* (who takes the garland), and on them lay the responsibility of bringing the wood upto the temple. When the specified *neem* tree is found, at first the dayitas will arrange for the bathing of the trees and garlanding them with the *ajnamalas* brought from the temple. When this ceremony is over they will abstain themselves from taking food and water for three days, and will sit in their temporarily built huts for meditation. The Brahmins for these three days will perform *yajnas,* invoking the deity one thousand and one hundred times. As there is no surety of getting all the trees at one place, the *yajnas* are arranged where the trees are available. On the last day after the full invocation, at first Pati Mahapatra with a golden axe, and then dayitapatis with silver axes, will touch the trees, after which the Vishwakarmas will start cutting down the trees. The main trunk is only required for modelling the image; other portion of the tree, including the twigs and the leaves, are buried under the earth. Then only preparation for taking the *mahadaru* (the holy wood) to Puri is taken up. Meanwhile, each trunk of the trees is covered with new red silken cloth, sprinkled with fragrance and garlanded profusely. These are kept on the respective bar rows, tied strongly with silken ropes. These barrows are mostly drawn by the people of the villages through which they pass, and that they do with blowing of conch shells, the playing of percussion instruments, and the singing of *kirtana* (devotional songs about Krishna). Within five to seven days these barrows reach the outskirts of the city of Puri, where the king waits to lead the procession with the playing of instrumental music to the north gate of the temple. Therefrom the woods are taken to the *darumandapa* (place for keeping these woods) inside the temple precincts. On the *snanyatra* day, after ablution of the woods are done with, the Savara Vishwakarmas start modelling the images. On that day the Brahmin priests commence *mahayajna* (great Yajna), at the commencement of which the king of Puri offers *ajnabastra* (a piece of cloth) to the chief Vishwakarma, and asks him to start the modelling work. While the modelling goes on inside the *nirmanamandapa* (place for modelling), nobody except the Pati Mahapatra and the Vishwakarmas are allowed to go there. The *yajna* continues for thirteen days, when amidst *kirtans* and loud sound of instrumental music the work of modelling continues. On the third day of the *Yajna*, shole fish (tubular fish) is sacrificed. Meanwhile, graves for the old images are prepared. The Brahmins, except those performing the *yajna,* join the activities from the twelfth day. On that day the chief priest hands over four small pieces of wood to Pati Mahapatra for repositing these in the navels of the deities, who then hand these over to the Vishwabasu (chief of dayitapatis), who then transmits them to the chief Vishwakarma for the purpose. Thirteenth day and the images are complete; at the same time full invocation at the *yajna* is also done. On this day the Brahmin priests and the Chief of the different monasteries can enter the nirmanaman-dapa; of course images at that time remain completely covered. The Rajguru and the priest touch the covered images with *kusa* (grass). All religious functions during the ceremony are done, ex-cepting chanting *kirtana,* according to the tantric customs. The invoking of the goddesses during the pre-nava kalevara period and the act of sacrificing fish in the *yajna* are customs followed by the Shaktas. These customs are taboo to the Vaishanavites. The next day, i.e. on the fourteenth day, a ceremony called *ghata paribartana* (changing of pots) is held. The new images are then brought inside the temple through *homa* (ablution of fire) and proper invocations, and these are placed face to face with the old ones. In the midnight of that day the *brahmamani* from inside the navel of the old deities are shifted to the new images, for which four eldest dayitapatis are summoned. Their eyes and hands are tied with thick cloth and the inside the temple is kept dark. Such precautions are taken as it is widely believed that seeing the *brahmamani* with open eyes and touching it with bare hands is a grave sin and it causes death. It is also said that at the time of transference of the *brahmamani* unforeseen natural calamities occur, for which soon after these are shifted, the priests perform *soroshapachara puja* (prayer with sixteen special articles for perfect worship) to pacify the god. No such happening during the shifting process has been so far reported.

After the placement of *brahmamani* inside the new images the dayitas bring out the images from the temple through the southern door to *Koili Vaikuntha* (graveyard named as such), and bury them in the prepared graves. Soon after, the dayitas start observing *asauch* (impurity). After observing asauch for eleven days they smear their bodies with oil at *muktimandapa* in the precincts of the temple, after which they go to nearby Markandeya *sarobara* (tank), where they shave themselves and take purificatory bath. After bath they wear new clothes given by the king, and become pure again. During this period the *dayitas* cry loudly, as is the custom of the Hindus to weep over the death of one in family. As the heirs of the deceased they have also claim over the property of the deceased. The temple authorities give them money on this account. In 1969, during such a function, the dayitas wer offered five thousand rupees *(The Cult of Jagannatha and the Regional Traditions of Orissa)*. The doors of the temple are not open in spite of the installation of the new images. The doors open after another ceremony, called *netrotsava* (netra means eyes, utsava is ceremony). After the *ghata paribartana* ceremony, new images are kept covered with silken cloth, when the painters wash the wooden images with chalk, and bring them to their natural forms with the painting work. After that the bodies of the figures are to be given 'flesh' and 'blood' by the Datta Mahapatras (they belong to the Kayastha community). This 'flesh' and 'blood' is nothing but shellac, lumps of sandal paste, pieces of silken cloth etc. So, we find that all the work about the new images till now being done by the Savaras and other low caste people, but what then is the role of the Brahmins except performing *yajnas*? Except Pati Mahapatra, the Brahmins specially appointed by the god through a divine commandment, as has been narrated in the "Myths and Legends" Chapter, the Brahmins have only one function before the temple doors are open for public. The function is to paint the eyes of the deities, which is called *netrotsava*. So, we find that during the nava kalevara, starting from the collection of wood to the cremation of the images, all works are done by the Savaras. After all, they are the beloved (dayitas) and relatives of Lord Jagannatha.

It has been stated earlier that the wood collected for the nava kalevara must have some special peculiarities. There are twelve direction in this matter, out of which four instructions have special significance. These are—1) There must be a Shiva temple near about the tree, 2) there should be a snake den under the tree, 3) there should be an ant-hill near the tree, and 4) there should be a cremation ground near the tree. Except the first named speciality, the other three completely contradict Hindu beliefs. In this connection the directions of Varahamihira is that those trees, which are near the confluence of rivers. near an ant-hill, near the cremation ground, and the tree under which there is a nest of snakes, should not be used in any auspicious work. Same directions have also been given by Marichi in Vimanachanakalpa. But in the selection of wood for Jagannatha and his companions, the directions are just the opposite of Hindu beliefs. It should also be noted that out of twelve directions, one is that there must be a Shiva temple near the tree. When it is held that the Jagannatha is the image of Sri Krishna, why does the Shiva temple gets such a priority? After looking at the activities and methods adopted during the nava kalevara ceremony, the pertinent point that manifests itself is that the Hindu beliefs have been grafted onto the religious beliefs and ideas of the primitive non-Aryans.

For assimilating a different faith into oneself, the diplomatic way is to do that slowly and as a continuing process. Here we find that after borrowing the gods and beliefs of the Savaras, Hindu rites were imposed slowly and steadily. Otherwise the Hindus would not have accepted such uncouth deities, and allowed aboriginal priests to worship them inside the temple.

It has been mentioned earlier that in certain parts of Orissa, aborogines worship Stambheshwari—in Oriya it is called Khambeshwari. As because it is also a log, which is perishable in course of time, they perform nava kalevara of Stambheshwari. Khonds, in particular, worship this deity. Like the Hindus they offer milk, fruits, rice, etc. to the deity. They also hear oracle for location of the tree, from which the image is to be built, and they also pray to the god before the tree is felled. Whereas in the Jagannatha temple on the third day of the yajna, when the images are being modelled, fish is sacrificed, Khonds sacrifice

an animal at the time of the prayer before the tree is felled.
Soon after the wood reaches the abode of the deity, adoration
of the new image starts after burning the old one. In the
Sonepur area of Western Orissa another tribe, Damals, also worship a log as their deity. These damals do not like to call
themselves tribals, preferring to be called as Hindu cultivators.
They have faith in worshipping *badi* (twigs and sticks assembled
and tied). They also arrange nava kalevara for their deity. In
fact, in most of the villages of western and southern Orissa the
log is being worshipped, and their pujas are being conducted by
their own priests. Like Stambheshwari, many such wooden deities
got royal patronage.

It has already been said that during the pre-Vedic times,
the non-Aryans were devotees of the Mother goddess and Shiva.
Yogiraj Pashupati, the Mother goddess, and bull figures of
Mohenjodaro give that indication. From the 6th century onwards
many gods and goddesses, who were being given supreme position in Hinduism, replacing the Vedic deities like Indra, Varuna,
etc., originated from the religious beliefs of the non-Aryans. The
goddesses like Uma, Kali, Durga, etc. are actually disguised
forms of the non-Aryan mother goddess. Matriarchal as they
were, worshipping the mother goddess was prevalent among the
primitives. Besides, for the fertility of the land they performed
magic and sacrificed animals before their deities. The transformation of the gods and goddesses in India was not an accident.
As Hinduism developed, in course of time, as an admixture of
Aryan and non-Aryan cultures, such transformation also took a
long time. It is because of possessing the quality of eclectism
that Hinduism could assimilate other religious beliefs into its fold.
It seems that the idea of God being all-pervading and om-
nipotent, because of which God can reveal himself everywhere,
and that whoever takes brith in this land is to be recognised
as Hindu, these two ideas helped Hinduism enormously to easily
assimilate other contradictory beliefs. The effects of such cohesive
attempts on the part of the Aryans with the beliefs of the primitives have yielded results. This process accelerated during the
post-Buddhist period resulting in the complete integration of those
assimilated elements into Hinduism. In spite of radical differences
in the beliefs of the primitives and that of the Aryans, that
difference started waning during this span of time. What happened to Buddhism? At one time Buddhist beliefs struck at the
root of Brahminism and made it impotent-like, lying prostrated
for a long time. Later, just for its survival's sake, Hinduism had
to accept the agnostic Buddha as their own *avatara* (god-incar-

nate). Though Jainism also struck at Aryan beliefs, its assault failed as it could not sufficiently infiltrate into the minds of the people. None of the Jaina Tirthankaras have been recognised as an *avatara* by the Hindus. In the pre-*Rg-Veda* era Aryans appointed people from among the primitives to act as their priests. These primitive priests were expert magicians. Pargiter in his book *Ancient Indian Historical Tradition,* D.D.Kosambi in his *An Introduction to the Study of Ancient History,* and R.S.Sharma in *Studies in Ancient India* have discussed much on the subject. In his article "Vedic Magic", A.A. Mcdonell has also said that before the composition of the *Rg-Veda* the magicians were elevated to the priesthood *(Encyclopaedia of Religion and Ethics).* In short, deciding to settle here permanently, the Aryans thought of not going against the local customs, and they settled for acceping a few native aristocrats and priests in their own community We come to know from the *Rg-Veda* of several sages whose colour of the body was black, like Angirasa Krishna and Satyakama Jabali, whose parenthood was not known, which indicates that the Aryans did not hesitate during the early period of their infiltration into India to give the leaders of those primitives the same position as their own. It can be assumed that for political reasons they accepted many things which they would not have normally done. That it was done for political purpose is clear, as we find that from the later part of the Rg-Vedic age, the ideas and precepts of the Aryans were not liberal, and that their attitudes were becoming sterner to other castes. The role of the Brahmins also changed. Caste division was enforced, allotting to the Brahmins supreme position in society, who were followed by the Kshatriyas. During the Mauryan age Hindu beliefs became sterner, and heredity was given importance. Kautilya advised the king to be vigilant for stopping cross-breeding. In other words, it can be said that a religious or political belief, however liberal is its pose before it can take its roots in the ground, exposes its true nature soon after its foundation is secure The Aryans, who in the initial stages, did not hesitate to recruit the primitives as their priests, in the later ages ridiculed and subdued them and branded them as *vanaras* (monkey) *pishachas* (evil spirit), *Rakshasas* (demons), etc.

In spite of the fact that those primitive tribes had many gods and goddesses, according to their own traditions, they were also devotees of Shiva and Shakti, as has been narrated in different scholarly works. From the writings of Banabhatta it is known that in the Vindhya mountain area Shakti was being worshipped in the name of Kiratini, Nagna Savari, etc. In the religious history of Orissa we find Mother goddesses like Vimala, Viraja, Mangala, Chamunda, who were being worshipped before the advent of Jagannatha. Sculptures of seven mother goddesses on the outer wall of the Shiva temples confirm the influence of Shaivism and Shaktism. It has been mentioned earlier that the Ganga dynasty treated Gokarneshwara of the Mahendra mountain, which was known to be the god of the Savaras, as their own god. Though Anantavarman Choraganga was known to be a Vishnuite, there is no such information that he desisted from worshipping the wooden god or Shiva. On the other hand, it is known that his wife Kasturikamodimi erected a temple at her birth place, Tekkali, on the east of Kalinganagara, Choraganga's first capital. She installed in it a wooden deity and arranged its adoration as Dadhivamana. According to some scholars the wooden deity known as Dadhivamana was once very much widespread, and that can be understood form the fact that even now there are 344 Dadhivamana images in Orissa.

Soon after ascending the throne, Choraganga had to face aggression from different quarters. He had to involve himself in war on the north-western side, wherefrom the Kalachuri king Ratnadeva the Second was attempting to invade Orissa, as also from the southern side of Kalinga, where the Cholas were attempting to gain control over the area on the Godavari coast. After successfully winning the wars, he, for keeping effective control of his kingdom, shifted his capital from the Kalinga side to Utkala at Sarangarh on the delta of the Mahanadi river near Cuttack. Before the Ganga rule over Orissa, Jajpur was known as Virajakshetra, Bhubaneswar as Shiva-kshetra, and Puri as Shakti-peetha, where Vimala is the Peetheshwari. The Gangas endeavoured to build up Puri as Purushottama-kshetra, and for that purpose planned to erect a massive temple. Like all other kings, Choraganga was adequately conversant with the fact that religion was the most valuable and effective weapon to win over the minds of the people. To eradicate any possibility of political explosion, he took shelter under religion. And with the temple there was the need of installing a deity, but which one? He opted for the wooden deity which was then occupying an important position among the aborigines at Puri. At that time Vaishnavism was spreading well over in Orissa. Choraganga desired an admixture of Nrisimha with the wooden deity there at Puri. History says that no king could maintain a kingdom for long, disregarding *lokachara* and *desachara* (local and village customs).

Choraganga was no exception to the rule. Whatever might have been his own religious beliefs, he declared the wooden deity as Nrisimha, and it is assumed that he did not dare to change the form of the deity. It is said that Ramanuja came to Puri when he was ripe in age to propagate Vaishnavism, and he could enlist Choraganga to his faith. After that what Ramanuja tried to do was to endeavour replacing the non-Aryan priests in the Puri temple with Brahmin priests, and to introduce there Brahminical rites and customs. But in spite of royal patronage, he had to cancel his plan and had to leave Puri during the darkness of night because of the terrible hostility of the non-Brahmin priests.

Shaiva-Shakta beliefs were most influential before the Ganga rule, as has been mentioned earlier. In the initial period of the Bhauma-Kara rule worshipping *Ekpada Bhairava* (Bhairava with one leg) was prevalent over an extensive area of Orissa. During the rule of the Kesari dynasty it was also prevalent. Even the Buddhists used to worship this Bhairava. On careful observation it would be noticed that there remains a similarity betwen Ekpada Bhairava and Jagannatha. It has been said that after initiation into Vaishnavism, Choraganga named Jagannatha as Nrisimha. This Nrisimha image is peculiar, as in it the human form and that of a lion is joined together. It seems that the idea of such a form could satisfy the aborogines. Nrisimha is a cruel form of Vishnu, as Bhairava is of Shiva. It should be noticed that Jagannatha was not directly termed as Vishnu at first; it was designated as Nrisimha, and later on as Purushottama. Till the Vashnavites could get absolute control over the temple affairs, the wooden deity was worshipped by the two communities, Shaivites and the Vaishnavites, according to their own respective customs. Here one small but significant incident needs mentioning. Before the Vaishnavites acquired complete control over the temple, Shaivism had enough influence there. It so happened that the followers of Samkara installed a Shiva idol along with an image of Samkara on the *ratnavedi* (jewel throne or platform) besides Jagannatha. (This jewel throne was plundered by the King Gajapati Purushottama Deva in 1489 after defeating the King of Vijayanagara and placed at the temple). Circa 1800 was the time when these two new figures

Ekpada Bhairava

needed reclamation, and the two forms were brought down from the platform for the purpose. But after reclamation, when these were being installed at the platform, the Vaishnavites did not allow the Shaivites to do so, which culminated in fights between the two religious communities. Ultimately the Vaishnavites got the upper hand, and they destroyed the two images and threw them into the sea. This incident indicates that the Vaishnavites, because of the royal patronage, secured the upper hand in the temple. Even then the priests of the temple were receiving their education in regard to the *pujas* of Jagannatha and about different ceremonies at the temple from the *Govardhana Matha* (Monastery founded by Samkara). Not only that, the Samkaracharya of the Govardhan matha of Puri had the authority of presiding over the necessary discussions at the *muktimandapa* of the temple relating to religious affairs (K.C. Mishra, *Cult of Jagannatha*). Moreover, even now Balabhadra is being worshipped according to the Shaivite rites and customs, and Subhadra and Vimala are being worshipped with Durga-Bhubaneshwari hymns (Shakti hymns).

Till the first part of the 12th century, Puri was known as Shivakshetra and Shakti-peetha. From the architectural styles of the temple of Kapalamochana, Yameshwara, Ishaneswara, Markendeshwara, etc., it can be assumed that these were erected during the Kesari rule. During the Ganga rule the most important Shiva temple of Puri was that of Markandeshwara. At that time there were two more temples dedicated to Nilakantha Shiva and Lokenatha Shiva, of which Nilakantha seems to be comparatively new. Though from the structure of the Lokenatha temple it also seems to be comparatively new, but from its location much inside the ground level it can be assumed that for this old deity a new temple was constructed on the older one. This Lokenatha is called "Prime Minister of Jagannatha". He participates on behalf of Jagannatha during the Chandan Yatra (one of the Lord's many *yatras*) festival. As regards Lokenatha's antiquity this much can be said that all the five principal Shiva temples of Puri face westwards. Whereas Hindu temples face east or south, the temples facing west were constructed during the Sailodbhava rule. No west-facing temple was constructed during the rule of the later dynasties. As regards the temple of Nilamadhava, as has been narrated in the myths, the location has still not been determined. It is difficult to determine as there was no temple in actuality. The Savara, Vishwabasu, had been worshipping Nilamadhava in the jungles in a small hut.

According to W.W. Hunter there are, out of ancient

temples in Puri, several Shiva temples and sixteen images of Shakti in different forms. He has specially mentioned the following Shiva temples—Yameshwara, Visheshwara, Kapalamochana, Markandeshwara, Nilakantheswara, Trilochana, Bhuteshwara, and Pataleshwara and the Shakti temples of Vimala, Mangala, Kali, Sarvamangala, Dhatri, Bhabani, and Ardha Asti. Amongst these he thought the temple of Yameshwara was the oldest, and that it was constructed in the eighth century. One criterion for determining the antiquity of the temple is its depth below the ground level. Yameshwara temple is down by 45 feet, Pataleshwara by 27 feet, whereas Ishaneshwara, Markandeshwara, and Kapalamochana by 61 feet. From the location of Ishaneshwara and Pataleshwara temples inside the precincts of the Jagannatha temple. it can be assumed that the temple which Yayati Kesari built was also at such a low level. Due to physical reasons and accumulation of sand deposits in course of time the ground level has come up. The sea has now moved away quite at a distance. At that time the sea was very near the temple, for which the temple could not stand long due to the salinity. It should be noted here that as the Lokenatha Shiva is called Prime Minister and Treasurer of Jagannatha, so the Ishaneshwara Shiva is called "maternal uncle of Jagannatha". As Virajakshetra at Jajpur, or Shivakshetra at Bhubaneswar has antiquity, so has Puri, which is mentioned in different Sanskrit texts, but as Purushottamakshetra it is comparatively new. That Puri was Shivakshetra and Shaktipeetha can be seen from the old *sloka* (verse) *"Vimala Bhairavi Yatra/Jagannathastu Bhairava"* It came to be known as Purushottamakshetra only after it came under the dominance of the Vaishnavites. It should here be specifically noted that Orissa, according to the scriptures, is the only state in India where all the five holy kshetras are assembled— Bhubaneswara as Shivakshetra, Jajpur as Shaktikshetra and Ganeshakshetra, Konark as Arkakshetra (Suryakshetra), and the present day Puri as Purushottamakshetra.

In the different inscriptions from the time of Anantavarman Choraganga, for several generations the name of Jagannatha is not found. We find Jagannatha as the God of Puri from King Bhanudeva the Second's Sriluram second inscription (1309) and from the Simhachalam inscription (1319). In the year 1230, during the rule of the King Anangabhima Deva the Third, the Shiva image amongst the Trinity became known as Balabhadra. In the Utkala part of the *Skanda Purana,* Balabhadra has been mentioned as 'Kalagni Rudra' and 'Maha Rudra' (Namah Kalagnirudraya Maharudraya te namah). From the Daksharama inscription of Anangabhima Deva the Third it is known that he declared himself as the son of the three images *(Sri Purushottama-putra, Rudra-putra, Durga-Putra*—son of Purushottama, i.e. Vishnu, son of Rudra, i.e. Shiva, and son of Durga, i.e. Shakti). After about fifteen years from the date of the above named inscription he declared himself as the son only of Purushottama, which means that by that time Vaishnavites were able to have full control over the temple activities. It was during his reign that the Jagannatha cult became supreme, though the image still then was known as Purushottama.

The image known as that of Subhadra is being worshipped with *Durga-Bhubaneshwari* hymns.   Referring to this image, Anangabhima Deva called himself as Durga-putra.   In the Purushottama-Mahatmya part of the *Skanda Purana,* Subhadra has been mentioned as the image of Lakshmi.   It should be noted here that this image is placed on the left side ·of Balabhadra. If it had been the image of Lakshmi, it should have been placed, according to the Hindu customs, on the left side of Jagannatha, who is treated as representing Vishnu.   Would it be wrong if we call it as representing Stambheshwari of the aborigines ?   All the three images have been modelled more or less in the same fashion, and when Jagannatha has now been recognised to be a Savara deity in origin, it is not unnatural to presume that to appease the important segment of tribal groups like the Khonds, etc., Stambheshwari was modelled before the Gangas cam to power. After all, the aborigines have implicit faith in Shakti, and Stambheshwari is nothing but a replica of Shakti.

In this connection it should also be noted that as in Puri so in Bhubaneswar the Savaras are treated as companions and attendants of Lingaraja. In the Lingaraja temple also there are two types of priests—Brahmin priests and Savara priests, who are known as Barus. On them fall the responsibility of arranging ablutions and dressing of the deity. During the festivities a deity representing Lingaraja is brought out for the purpose of traversing the city.   It is called the *Chalanti pratima* (mobile god), and on the Barus falls the responsibility of carrying it.   It is common belief that if the Barus are not there, the god will not move an inch.   The present Lingaraja temple was erected in the 9th century during the reign of the Kesaris.   From *Ekamra Purana* it is known that the deity was found by the aboriginal Savaras from beneath a mango tree.   According to the said Purana this deity was not visible in *Satya* or *Treta Yugas* (the first and second ages of the world according to the Hindus), and it exposed itself as the image of a *lingam* (phallus) during *Dwapara* and *Kali Yugas* (third and fourth ages), but as there was no temple there the Savaras used to worship it beneath a mango tree. This *Purana* further says that the Barus are an offshoot of the Savaras, who had been living there and worshipping the god beneath the tree. When Sasanka, the king of Karnasuvarna, occupied the territory, he identified the figure and erected a temple for regular *puja* of the *lingam*. Sasanka was an ardent devotee of Shiva, and he built the first Lingaraja temple, which got destroyed, on the edifice of which Yayati Kesari raised the present magnificent temple. As in Puri here also, under the influence of the Vaishnavites, the temple is no longer of *Hara* (Shiva), it has now become *Harihara* (Hari is Vishnu, Hara is Shiva); the image of the *lingam* is not now visible. What is visible is a figure of *OM* (a mystic sound indicating the Hindu Trinity) and a snake, which is taken to be a companion of Shiva. It should be noted that here also the Savara priests were appointed by the King Yayati Kesari.

On reviewing all the aspects, it seems that the four-fold images in the Jagannatha temple today commonly known as that of Balabhadra, Subhadra, Sri Krishna, and Sri Sudarshana had been so named during the later part of the Surya dynasty's rule. This change had been made possible by the efforts of Jayadeva, Ballavacharya, and Sri Chaitanya. The sum and substance of this is that the wooden deity of the Savaras was named differently in various periods through the sheer force of publicity carried out by different religious communities. Thus originated names like Dadhivamana, Patitapavana, Nrisimha, Purushottama, Jagannatha, and Sri Krishna. From this simple fact of distorting a deity with different names at different periods, it can be understood what command and impact the contemporary religious beliefs can impart on the minds of the people. And royal patronage for such religious beliefs had always been there. So, it has to be found out what the actual deity was, difficult though this is as too much confusion has been created by the religionists.

It has already been stated that this Jagannatha culture has assimilated into itself all the Indian religious beliefs, that Jagannatha reveals himself in five forms of different gods and goddesses, and that in the practices and hymns of the *pujas* all Indian religious beliefs are manifested. Taking everything into consideration it must be said that the religious culture that has grown around Jagannatha is not only unique, it is great. To make this culture more glorious it is essential that the doors of the temple should be kept wide open for all human beings. Only then will this Jagannatha culture be recognised as the representative of all Indian religious beliefs.

NRISIMHA

CHAPTER IX

SUMMING UP

IT HAS been said in the preceding chapter that around this mystic Lord Jagannatha, a new religious culture has evolved, which is unprecedented in this country of religious strifes and conflicts. It will be appropriate for the religionists to take the cue from the Jagannatha culture to co-exist peacefully. There is no doubt that religious chauvinism begets ill feelings between man and man, which, again, ultimately unsettles the stability of a nation.

It has been remarked earlier that because of its quality of eclecticism, Hinduism could take into itself many aspects of other religious beliefs. True to that spirit of the ages, Puri's Jagannatha has assimilated all the religious beliefs in itself. Still then, the sense of discrimination between man and man through castes and classes are strong enough. Religionists speak for caste, and politicians for class distinction. When the deities of the non-Aryans and of the depressed classes are being Hinduised, when Gautama Buddha, the celebrated atheist, could be recognised to be one of the god-incarnates, when Satyapira of the Muslims could be transformed to Satyanarayana of the Hindus, it is a matter of great regret and worry that even now non-Hindus and low caste Hindus are not allowed entry into many Hindu temples. It was to demand entry into the temple of all people, irrespective of class, caste, or creed, that Gandhiji organised *satyagraha* in front of the Jagannatha temple. The late Prime Minister Indira Gandhi could not even get permission from the temple authorities to enter the temple. This author has noticed that whereas an elephant is not debarred from entering the Vishnu temple at Kanjeevaram, a non-Indian was not allowed that facility. An hour-long *satyagraha* by this author in front of that temple in protest against one such incident in 1977 or 1978, not allowing a non-Indian to enter the temple, proved fruitless—he got boos instead. Such examples are many. It is particularly perplexing to note that when the management of the Jagannatha temple is now under the control of the State Government of Orissa, the doors of the temple are not yet open to the non-Hindus and low caste Hindus. It is indeed a pity that even the Saoras, who are still maintaining their separate identity, are not allowed entry into the temple, and that in spite of the fact that Jagannatha has now been recognised to be a Savara deity in origin.   Is this not a case of nexus between religion and politics ?

While going back to the discussion we have noticed that Shiva Shakti influence on the minds of the people was dominant since ancient times, and that King Yayati Kesari of the Soma dynasty was an ardent Shaivite. Did he then install the icons of Shiva and Shakti when he built the temple at Puri along with the image of the wooden deity ? Nothing about it is found in the inscriptions left by the Soma Kings. From the Nagpur inscription of 1104 and the Govindpur inscription of 1137 it is known that at that time there was one specific image, which was known as Purushottama. It is also known from an inscription of 1225, carved on the temple of Pataleshwara in the precincts of the Jagannatha temple complex, that during the reign of Anangabhima Deva the Third, offerings were made only to Purushottama. Again, from another inscription of 1236, scrawled on the same temple, it is understood that offerings were being made to Halin, Chakrin, and Subhadra (*Epigraphica India*, Vol. 30, p.202). Shall we then assume that the other two images, that of Halin and Subhadra, were placed on the sanctum some time during 1225 and 1236? Or, that two images were there from earlier times, but due to the predominance of one particular religious belief these were ostracised? And what about the original wooden deity, now called as Sri Sudarshana - was it not there then? Another question crops up - if the icons of Balabhadra and Subhadra are those of Shiva and Shakti, then which god does Jagannatha represents—Vishnu, Sri Krishna, or any other ? What was the form of the original deity - present form of Jagannatha, or just a log like Sudarshana ? Whatever be the time of changing the form and name of the god, the manifestation of that log has found a place on the *ratnavedi* and it is also being worshipped five times a day. This log performs some important role, as it is recognised to be the *chalanti pratima* of Jagannatha. On the eighth day of the bright moon in the month of Bhadra (August-September), this mobile god is to traverse the city. During the *rathayatra* as also during *nava kalebara* when the party goes to the jungle in search of the neem trees, this log gets the priority of leading the procession. The belief is ingrained that this log will make the journey easy and smooth. At the time of collecting the woods, the tree for this icon is at first selected, and the *ajnamala* meant for this deity remains not with the *dayitapatis* but with the *Pati Muhapatra*. Again, when *brahmamani* gets transferred to the new images from the old ones, first of all it is performed for this icon. This log measuring 84 x 21 *yaba* (1 *yaba* is 1/4 inch), properly clothed, gets its place on the left side of Jagannatha and receives its *puja*. The height of the other three images are - Jagannatha 84 *yaba,* Balabhadra 85 *yabas,* and Subhadra 52 yabas. So, we find that height of Jagannatha and Sudarshana to be the same. These two events look very small, but these are actually very significant. Whereas the shape of Sudarshana of Vishnu / Sri Krishna is of circular type, this Sudarshana is elongated. The myth about the circular wheel getting elongated has been stated in page 81, from which we can see to what lengths the imagination of the religionists go. That the story was based on pure and simple imagination needs no explanation. How will the religionists and the dogmatic political ideologues survive, if they do not fabricate such tales ? It should here be remembered that all the kings of Orissa upto the Ganga dynasty came from outside. There can be only one argument of placing and worshipping the log, and that is to keep the dominant aborigines in good humour. It was very easy for a king to remove it from the *ratnavedi*, but that would have created much trouble in maintaing peace and tranquility in the kingdom, and would not have served any political purpose. No king wanted to face the cacophony of unrest and agitation. Though the Hindu kings did install images according to their own faiths, they did not dare to stop the *puja* of this log. Due to the support and patronage of the Vaishnavites the log has been mamed as Sri Sudarshana, and, so, there was no need of removing it. It is conjectured that when the wooden deity was transformed to Jagannatha, this was also placed beside it. And that could appease the volatile Savaras. Hymns for worshipping Sudarshana are the Nrisimha hymns. Different Puranas have narrated the closeness of Sudarshana and Vishnu, and later with Sri Krishna. *Mahabharata* and *Padma Purana* say that this Sudarshana Chakra was created out of some parts of the Sun; *Samba Purana* says that Vishwakarma created it in imitation of the Sun; *Banchha Purana* says that Mahadeva handed the Sudarshana over to Vishnu for killing the demons; and, according to the Buddhists, this is Dhamma Chakra.

It has been stated earlier that aboriginal blood ran in King Yayati Kesari's veins. His mother was a Kshatriya. And as he wanted to be recognised as a Hindu, he performed several *Aswamedha Yajnas* (horse sacrifice), and also arranged for the settlement of many Brahmins in Orissa. After carefully considering all the available sources, it can be concluded that he was the first person to erect the Jagannatha temple at Puri, and it was he who accommodated the Savara *dayitas* for *pujas* in the temple along with the Brahmins. He should have been satisfied with installing Shiva and Shakti images, but as king it was his responsibility to keep the turbulent aborigines pacified. Otherwise, why had he to cry for the *"Odisa Rajara Prabhu"* and started searching extensively for it after he came to the throne of Orissa? Was there any need of searching another Lord, when he was a devotee of Shiva ? The Lord, who is supposed to have left Puri 144 years back, was after all recovered by him in a very much fragmented condition, near about his own birth place. This is also a significant point in this study The distinctive point is how could he know from the titbits of the wood found beneath a tree that it was that of the Lord, particularly when no picture of the Lord was available? Could these titbits indicate what was the original form of the Lord ? It was not possible. And so, disinformation was a necessity, for which myths and legends had to be manufactured. At that time the predominant religion of Orissa was Shaivism-Shaktism, and the king himself was a devout follower of that religious belief. From the various currents and cross-currents extant, it can be concluded that he modelled and installed the wooden deity along with the wooden log, in the patterns of the aborigines, purely out of political expediency. He must have also modelled the icons of Shiva and Shakti in the same model. One does not know what was the actual form of the idols at that time. It seems that the modelling of the images was changed in different times during the reign of the later dynasties, particularly when the images had to be shifted to hidden places a number of times, and after the images were burnt to ashes by Kalapahada. It has already been said that the Ganga king, Choraganga, named the Jagannatha image as Nrisimha, and after him another Ganga king, Ananga Bhima Deva, named it as Purushottama, when he made an attempt to remove the three other icons from the public eyes. It was he who in 1226 mentioned Purushottama as the one and only god, but he had to retreat under political pressure and had to rehabilitate the other three images in 1236, when these were named as Halin, Subhadra and *Darubrahma* (Sudarshana), and named Jagannatha as Chakrin. The next change must have occurred during the rule of the Solar dynasty, when we came across with the names, Balabhadra, Subhadra, Jagannatha, and Sri Sudarshana.

The temple erected by Yayati Kesari was in a dilapilated condition when the Ganga dynasty came to power. Choraganga Deva started re-building the temple on a grand scale, and it was completed by Ananga Bhima Deva. It has already been mentioned that during Choraganga Deva's rule, there was, under the initiative of Ramanuja, an attempt made to dispense with the duties of the Savara *dayitas* from the *pujas* in the temple. In spite of the fact that at that time these *dayitas* were no longer wild Saoras they were then Suddha (purified) Savaras. Ramanuja's attempt was to transform it to purely a Hindu temple. However, only if the exact form of the deities during the Keasari rule could have been known, the controversy could have been unravelled.

A peculiar point has been raised about the image of Jagannatha by William Bruton in his book *Newes from the East Indies* (Indian edition renamed as Bruton's Visit to Lord Jagannatha 350 Years Ago, edit. P.T. Nair, Minerva, Calcutta, 1985). He went to Puri in 1633, saw the image and *rathayatra*. He has remarked thus, "The Idoll is in the shape like a great serpent, with seven heads, and on the cheeks of each head it hath the forms of a Wing upon each cheeks, which wings doe open and shut, and flaps, as it is caried in a stately chariot, and the Idoll in the midst of it." About *rathayatra* he said that there were two chariots, and the main chariot had sixteen wheels, and it was of 30 ft. height. Was the image of Jagannatha made in this form 350 years ago ? It is true that from very ancient time the Snake god was being worshipped in India - it is also an aboriginal god, but it cannot be believed that in 1633 Jagannatha was being worshipped in the form of a snake with seven heads. That was the time when Muslim rule was there, and before and during their rule the idol had to be shifted from Puri on several occasions. In between 1590 and 1750 the image was shifted from Puri about twelve times, as there had been continuous threats of Muslim aggression. No document has been found from which we can come to know whether any other image was installed in the temple, when the idols were shifted. We only know that when Kalapahada destroyed the images, there was no idol at the temple. It might be that there was some such arrangement to hoodwink the aggressors. If that was so, Bruton in 1633 may have seen such figure. But what he has written about *rathayatra* can be rejected, as he saw this festival in the month of November, whereas it occurs in the month of June-July. As he had no knowledge about the Oriya language, he had to take help of the local inhabitants. Bruton was a foreigner, and that was a time when the threat of Muslim aggression was in the air. It might be that panic-stricken people hesitated to speak the truth to a foreigner, and told him some fantastic stories. There is also a possibility that some groups

Jagannatha's chariot festival as seen and sketched
by William Bruton in 1633

organised *Naga Puja* (serpent worship), and they organised a
procession. Moreover, he saw two chariots only, whereas at that
time there were three images, besides Sudarshana, who has no
chariot. This is a guess work, and it would be wise to make
further inquiries into the matter before we come to a conclusion.

When Yayati Kesari built the Lingaraja temple at Bhubaneswar, and made the land known as Shivakshetra, why did he
build another temple at Puri ? Firstly, all the kings at that time
knew very well that to receive spontaneous welcome and
glorification from the population at large, the simplest way was
to erect temple and instal gods. Secondly, Puri and its neigh-

bouring areas were habitats of the Savaras and other tribes. The cooperation of the people would have been easily available by building a temple-oriented civilization. This was known to Yayati Kesari, who was very much in need of cooperation of the Hindus as well as of the Savaras and other aborigines. And Hindu civilization is indeed a temple-oriented civilization. For planting utopian beliefs into the minds of the people, the temple was the best medium. It seems Yayati Kesari did not have to face trouble in building Puri on the sea coast as a holy place, and built not only the temple, but also installed images of gods that were popular among the people.

As the name of the original deity changed different times under the influence of the prevailing religious cults, a clearer picture as to the original nature of the god in whose image the icons were made is not in hand, except the conclusion to which the scholars agree that is was originally a wooden deity of the Savaras. But which deity of the Savaras, particularly when they also have a plethora of gods and godesses? Ramma-Bimma-Sitaboi or Manjurasam Kittung, the Lord of Puri? This author thinks that it was the unrefined image of Uyungsun, that is the Sun god of the Savaras and of other aborigines. Due to the intensity of leprosy and skin diseases among the aborigines, they, for getting cured of these diseases, worship the Sun god, who is supposed to help them in the matter. Leprosy is well spread in the lower Ganges valley, in the coastal area of the Eastern and Southern India, and especially at the foot of the Vindhyas the districts of Puri, Koraput, Bolangir, Sambalpur, Ganjam, and neighbouring areas of Andhra Pradesh and Madhya Pradesh. Besides the Savaras, others amongst the Kolarian groups of peoples like Mundas, Santhals, etc. also worship the Sun god to get rid of the curse of this disease. Why only the aborigines, worshipping the Sun god is much in vogue in the country as well as in the other parts of the world, and though idols of Sun god are not being installed now, Sun worship still continues. Hindus are no less Sun worshippers. The Kesari dynasty was also no exception to it, which can be gauged from the Barahanath temple at Jajpur and the Lingaraja temple at Bhubaneswar, about which mention has been made in preceding chapters. There is a Sun temple in the precincts of the Jagannatha temple. Moreover, on the Orissa temples *nabagraha* (nine planets) images are carved, and the Sun bears a close relationship with *nabagrahas*.

But if Jagannatha be taken to be the Sun god, why has it been painted black, whereas other two images are painted white and golden? In ancient Sanskrit literature it has been stated that the Sun bears twosome colour - sometimes it is boundless white, sometimes it is black and dark. Moreover, its rays have different colours. In the *Rg-Veda* we find the following sloka: *"Tanmitrasya Barunasyabhichaksha/surya rupam brinute dourupatha/Anantamnyadrushadasya Pujah Krishnamnanga Harita-Suryasya."* The two-fold colour of the Sun has also been mentioned in the *Chhandogyasruti*. The Savaras paint their deities with black colour. And Jagannatha originally was a Savara deity.

But when did Jagannatha become Sri Krishna? In the religious history of Orissa, the names of Sri Ramachandra or Sri Krishna were not much heard at the early stages. During the rule of the Solar dynasty Sri Krishna crept in with the help of Jayadeva, Ballavacharya, and Sri Chaitanya. But these changes from the Ganga period were not smoothly effected. In the post-Yayati era the Ganga dynasty and the Solar dynasty had to face enough troubles, which mainly emanated from the priests of the temple, and occasionally from the aborigines. Anangabhima Deva of the Ganga dynasty wanted his Purushottama to be the one and only god to be worshipped in the temple, but he had to bow down before popular pressure and accept Halin and Subhadra as well. Chaitanya was slighted by the priests of the temple; and why slighted only, he had to die. Chaitanya could sense the hostility of the priests. It must have dawned on him that he might have to face a physical catastrophe, for which he never traversed the *ratnavedi*, nor did he enter inside the main temple. He, of course, used to visit the temple complex daily, and standing near the *Garuda Stambha* (pillar of Garuda, the mythical name of a bird) just outside the door of the main temple he had been viewing and praying to his god. After the death of Chaitanya the Gaudiya Vaishnavites had to flee away from Puri and they did not return to that city for quite some time. Not only Chaitanya, even the Solar King Prataparudra Deva was ridiculed. There was a conspiracy around his throne, and the conspirators were several high ranking officers of the king and a section of the priests of the temple. They were hand in glove with each other. Soon after the death of Prataparudra Deva, who was then broken in mind and spirit, his two sons were put on the throne successively but both of them were murdered within days. The leader of the conspirators was Govind Vidyadhara, who thereafter usurped the throne, and paved the way for annihilating Orissa's glorious heritage. When Prataparudra Deva was fighting against his enemies on two fronts of his kingdom, it was this Vidyadhara who betrayed the king and maligned him.

Vishnuites beliefs remained stationery in the southern part
f Kalinga for a long time. It was only since the 11th century
at their sphere of influence spread to the main parts of Kalin-
a and Utkala. It is the law of history that one royal dynasty
nnot remain in power for all the time. With time, new and
wer dynasties come to power. The same law also relates to
e Hindu gods and goddesses. As the king is the representative
 the gods, so gods and goddesses also depend on the rulers'
mpathy and consideration. *"Rajanugata Dharmah"* (Religion
eys the king). The earliest Aryan gods like Indra, Varuna (sea
d), etc. are not worshipped now, excepting, of course, Surya
d Agni, who have some important place in Hindu rituals. In
ct, without these two gods, no Hindu ritual is complete. There
ere no anthropomorphic gods during the Vedic days. Nature in
 different forms was then invoked through *yajna*. Brahma was
cognised to be the creator of everything, and he was called
andfather. This grandfather is no longer in the minds of the
ople, or being worshipped. Similarly, where is Indra now
at all-powerful god of the Aryans? He is no longer in the
cture. During post-Vedic days, in fact in Pauranic days, new
ds and goddesses emerged in the Hindu pantheon. The gods,
ose followers were zealously carrying propaganda, got
engthened. Vishnu is comparatively new, but, in course of
ne, Vishnu became the most powerful god. Earlier he was only
e of the adityas. Now-a-days, we hear of a film goddess,
ose appearance was sudden; but with what a terrific speed
e has conquered the hearts of the people with the help of the
ver screen. This goddess is Santoshi Ma, who has even
cured a corner at the Lingaraja temple. No small wonder, in-
ed ! Whatever that might be, apart from having some place
 the day-to-day Hindu rituals, it is in vogue that prayer to
 Rising Sun has to be made before starting other activities
 the Jagannatha temple complex. It may also be mentioned
re that the principal festivities of South India, Pongal, and
hat pujah of Bihar and neighbouring places are actually fes-
ities to worship the Sun god.

Another question comes in here - why Subhadra along with
labhadra and Sri Krishna, i.e. Jagannatha? If Sri Krishna is
 first deity, why is not Radhika there, who was and is in-
arably connected with Sri Krishna? *Kirtans* are sung in the
nes of Radha and Krishna. Why then Subhadra, who is not
ognised as a Hindu goddess? The only rational answer is that
 image was installed there before the Vaishnavites got control
er the affairs of the temple. There might have been a desire

to remove it, but that could not be done again for politica
reasons. As the Hindu mind is too much attuned to super
naturalism, no pains were spared to convince the believers t
accept Subhadra as a goddess. Here lies the skill and efficienc
of the religious communities, who are votaries of Krishna.

On the other hand, we know that Jagannatha takes fiv
different forms of different gods on occasions, but he does nc
take the form of Sri Krishna. These five forms are   he i
Narayana on the *ratnavedi*, Ganesha during *snanyatra*, Rudra a
the time of *nava kalevara*, Durga when he goes to the bec
and Surya-Narayana at the time of *rathayatra*. R.K. Das in hi
book *Legends of Jagannatha, Puri,* states that : "The tantric cor
ceives Balabhadra as Tara, Subhadra as Bhubaneswari, and Jagar
natha as the presiding deity of Shyama Tantra. Sanatan Brahmir
relate Balabhadra to Mahadeva, Subhadra to Durga, and Jaga
natha to Vishnu, and Sudarshana to Sun." Amidst all the jou
neys of the Lord, *rathayatra* is the most important. This is th
journey which he himself takes; others are made by his repr
sentatives.   Actually, the idols are brought out from the *ra
navedi* twice a year, during *snanyatra* and *rathayatra*. Naturall
it is recognised to be the most important festival. In this festiva
the role of the Savaras is significant. The deities are dressed i
Savara fashion with waist bands, etc., before they are placed c
the chariots. *Dayitas* also dress themselves with waist bands an
recite poems on the chariots. According to the Hindu custom
the auspicious direction for the journey is to the eastern sid
whereas with the Savaras it is north-east. It should be noted th
Shiva is the presiding deity of that corner. During the *rathayatr*
a section of *sevayets* (priests), called Dahukas, dance on t
verandah of the chariots and sing obscene songs. It is the beli
of the Savaras that as the malevolent gods and goblins cann
withstand obscenity, they will not create obstacles in the journe
Besides, before placing the deities on the chariots, the *dayit.*
tie them with specially prepared amulets, consisting of vario
creepers, leaves and roots of trees. This is actually a tantr
talisman prepared for safeguarding the bodies of the deities fro
evil.

It has been earlier stated that during the Ganga rule f
some time till 1235 A.D. only one deity, that of Purushottam
was recognised, and a stony silence was maintained about t
other deities; all of a sudden in the year 1236 Halin and Su
hadra got back their seats on the *ratnavedi*. Why? That is
million dollar question to be thought over. A little discussion

is point is called for. King Anangabhima Deva the Third (211-1245) was ruling over the then Orissa. He was the first anga King, who declared himself as the representative of urushottama. From the records available, it is found that after e decline of the Soma dynasty, the Sambalpur-Sonepur-Bolangir rea was occupied by the Kalachuris, who were descendants of e Haihaya dynasty. Choraganga's attempts to occupy this area f Western Orissa failed, as he had to come back time and gain being defeated at the hands of the Kalachuris. It was circa 236 that Anangabhima Deva could occupy the area, the decisive lace of which was Seori-Narayana (the legend about this village as been told earlier). And again, this is the same Western Oris-a, wherefrom King Yayati Kesari recovered the deity in a frag-ented condition after 144 years. This is the area where primi-ve tribes like Savaras, Khonds, etc. have been maintaining ominating influence for millennia. And this is the area where ujas of the deformed Kittungs and of Stambheshwari were well pread. King Anangabhima Deva must have been in a very much mbarrassing situation, as he had then been facing threats of ag-ression from the Kalachuris in the west, and from the Muslims the north. He must have then taken recourse to pacify the rimitives of Western Orissa for getting their cooperation and elp in his wars. And he must have felt that the best way to ucceed in this effort was to re-introduce Halin and Subhadra. rom the trends of the situation it will not be irrational to con-ude that the king was compelled by the objective condition to habilitate the two deities, who were very near to the poriginals' beliefs. Dr. Sukumar Sen, the celebrated philologist, an article (*Aajkal*, Bengali dialy, 3.7.81) holds that out of the ree deities Subhadra is the most ancient. His opinion can per-aps be pooh-poohed by some. It is also the considered opinion f this author that this Shakti image, now called Subhadra, is e oldest amongst the three, and that King Yayati Kesari in-alled along with it the figures of Shiva and of Uyungsum of e Savaras, the log being also kept there as a symbol. The ructural pattern and the design do not conform with Hindu leas, whereas they are in consonance with the Savara conception f the figures. In the Chapter on "Myths and Legends" it has en narrated that the temple built by the mythical King In-adyumna got buried under the sand, and the horse of the King alamadhava stumbled upon it. When the sands were removed, ing Galamadhava found that the top of the temple was a tri-nt. Does not that story indicate that the temple was actually Shiva-Shakti? And, Alviella (earlier said) thinks that the figure Jagannatha is the symbol of *trisula* (trident).

It is saddening to think that when on one side science
helping to enlarge the vision and thought processes of huma
beings, on the other hand attempts to establish "truth" based
falsehoods are being vigorously propagated to curb independe
thinking. It has been noticed that throughout the ages effecti
initiative has always been taken by the religionists and politic
dogmatics to stifle free thought. The course of a river can
changed by erecting a dam over it, but that cannot suppress
movement. Similarly, when beliefs, based on imagination a
taradidles, are placed on the touchstone of scientific analys
these get razed to the ground. Human beings are essential
emotional, and that is based on a biological factor. As t
religionists and the political fanatics want to control the majori
of a society, they are generally adept in exploiting that fact
of the human being. To arouse the emotion to a higher pit
they will titillate the sense organs of the people by manufactu
ing imaginary tales ; and, ultimately, in course of time, the
stories are purported to be history pieces. Hypes and hyperbol
have a great role to play in support of those religionists a
politicians. Emotion is one of the instincts that man shou
possess. But it has two aspects—positive and negative. In t
field of creation, emotion has a big role to play, if it is a
companied by reason; but when only emotion alone is allow
to play, it brings in disaster, at least it paves the way to th
That religion ultimately falls into the trap of communalism
very much visible in this country, and that is the result of em
tional upsurge, where reason does not count. A vigil is bei
constantly maintained by those vested interests, comprising of t
religionists and the politicians, as they are always in or near t
corridor of political power, so that people's thinking does r
get mixed up with rationalism. That is why they sneer at the
who speak of scientific and rational thinking. They are awa
that if rationalism gets a place to play in man's thinki
process, the castles that they have built up on sands of hyp
and hyperboles by playing on the soft emotion of the peop
will crumble down. Though methods are not always the san
there is close relation between the religionists and politicians.
establish the real truth, a rational and scientific mind is absolu
ly essential. And then and then only the so-called "truth" bas
on mendacity will be recognised as untruth. However pain
and ornamented these are, untruth is untruth and it cannot
transformed into truth.

In fact, the main purpose of this discussion is an atten
to find out the truth from the misty mythological misinformati

It should be remembered that falsehoods are not the monopoly of the Aryans or Hindu religion; all kinds of religious beliefs throughout the world very much depend on untruth, and they spread mists over the facts to serve their ulterior purpose. And we call this process supernaturalism—super and naturalism, that which is not natural.

We reach the following conclusions from this discussion :

I. The original wooden deity was in earlier times being worshipped by the wild primitives, known as Saoras or Savaras. For their own political interests, it was plundered by the rulers and brought to Puri. In course of time it was accepted as a Hindu god.

II. Out of the three deities, Subhadra is the oldest. This is not surprising, as since . pre-historic times the worship of Shakti was very much prevalent   this image is none other than the pre-Vedic Mother goddess.

III. King Yayati Kesari, according to his religious belief, installed a Shiva figure (now known as Balabhadra); and for political purpose he installed the figure of Uyungsun (Sun god) along with representative of the original wooden deity, which is now revered as Sri Sudarshana. Thus he could keep the Savaras and the other tribes in good humour.

IV. The wooden deity of the Savaras was alloted a dignified position to keep them satisfied;   and the Savaras were recognised as the relatives and sevakas of the Lord.

V. The deity was shifted, after its installation, from Puri, not once, but several times.   King Yayati Kesari, according to the legends, recovered the deity in a very much fragmented condition from beneath a tree in Western Orissa, where it remained, it is told, interred for 144 years.   The inner meaning of the myth is that Yayati Kesari, for his own political purposes, brought the Savaras with him from Western Orissa along with the parts of the wooden deity of the Savaras for modelling the image, and for taking charge of serving the deities along with the Brahmin priests.

VI. The wooden deity was named differently at different times.   During Ganga rule, it was first known as Nrisimha, and then as Purushottama.   The deities were named Balabhadra, Sub-hadra, Jagannatha/ Sri Krishna, and Sri Sudarshana during the rule of Solar dynasty kings.   Of course, Ganga King, Anangab-hima Deva, named Shiva as Halin, and Shakti or Durga as Sub-hadra.

VII. Jagannatha is extolled as a form of five different gods and goddesses   as Narayana on the *ratnavedi*, Ganesha during *Snanyatra*, Durga at the time of going to the bed, Rudra during *nava kalevara*, and Sun during *rathayatra*.   In other words, dif-ferent Indian religious beliefs have been synthesized into one image.   Notable fact is that in these important functions nowhere Sri Krishna has been mentioned.

VIII. As leprosy was very much widespread among the primitive tribes, they used to worship the Sun god, who was known to them as Uyungsun, for getting cured of it; and the Sun god is supreme among them.   The image was modelled by the Savaras with *neem* wood.   *Neem* leaves and juice of the tree are supposed to contain medicinal properties for curing leprosy and skin diseases.   Moreover, the *neem* tree has a close relation with the Sun.   And so, it is considered that the icon of Jagannatha is counterpart of the Savara god, Uyungsun.

IX. All the deities are modelled according to the artistry of the Savaras.   To pacify the wild Saoras and to keep them happy Uyungsun was accepted later on as the main deity.

X. The theory that it is a Vaishnava temple can safely be ruled out.   To legitimise their control over the temple affairs, they manufactured several myths to mystify the people at large. Moreover, if the life-substance *(brahmamani)* is to be treated as Lord Krishna's bone, the question arises - does Vaishnavism per-mit a human bone to be inserted in an image?   Needless to say that the introducion of a human bone into a Hindu image is opposed to the rules and cannons of Brahminical Hinduism.

APPENDIX

A SHORT HISTORY OF THE TOWN OF PURI OR JAGANNATH
By W.H. Lee

1st edition, Cuttack, Printed at the Orissa Mission Press, 1808 (W.H Lee in his Preface to this tract containing 16 pages in English, Oriya, and Bengali with a map, says: "The translations were made by Babu Bhagabati Charan Sen, Deputy Inspector of Schools, Puri District", Puri, November 25, 1807. English text runs to 6 pages only)

HISTORY OF THE TOWN OF PURI

/1/ Puri must have been an important town-doubtless chosen for its salubrious climate, proximity to the sea fishing, and healthy sandy soil—in the days before the Aryan invasion.

We unfortunately have no materials for the history of those days, but the Mahabharata speaks of Orissa as an ill-favoured tract lying between the mouths of the Ganges and the Krishna, covered with dense jungles, hemmed in by ranges of impassable mountains to the North, West and South, and inhabited by savage jungle tribes named Sabars and Kandhs. Doubtless with them were associated the ances-/2/tors of the present Pans, Bauris, Doms and Haris of Orissa. After the establishment of the Aryan kingdoms, and the systematisation of the various tribes and half-castes according to the Hindu social scheme, we find the inhabitants of this province took notice of the ancient aboriginal worship by the Sabars of a blue stone in the forest at Puri town, and making a wooden image and calling it Jagannath, gathered sufficient sentiment around it to make it a financial success, and to erect a temple to it, and finally to make Orissa a sacred country. From this time on we have the palm-leaf records of the temple, but our present edition is (like many other sacred books) a late redaction and the first part is purely mythical. We touch history at a series of invaesions from the North by Yavanas or Graeco Bactrians from B.C. 538 to 421. These pillagers brought Buddhism with them, and Puri became a great Buddhist strong-hold. The Jagan-/3/nath temple was pulled down, or waned into insignificance. Buddha's tooth was brought to Puri in 543 B.C. and taken away subsequently to Ceylon, where reliable records of the event are kept in the Singhalese sacred Pali text.

In 319 and 323 we have accounts of the descend upon the
town of Puri of piratical hordes from the Sea under the
leadership of one "Rakta Bahu" or "Red-arm". These men entered
the town, pillaged the temple, and killed the King and those of
the inhabitants who did not flee in terror. Who they were
nobody knows, but they are called Yavanas, and, as they brought
horses and elephants with then in their ships, were probably
either Graeco-Baktrian adventurers from the Ganges, or pirates
from Asia Minor, the Red Sea, or Germany, going up the coast
and ravaging as they went. The nickname "Rakta-Bahu" may
have been given to the leader/4/ because he had a red arm, or
more probably on account of his ruthless deeds. Anyhow these
pirates liked Puri so much that after their second invasion they
settled down in it; and they and their descendants held the land
for 150 years. Of this occupation, beyond an entry or two in
the palm leaf records (which were not maintained during the
foreign rule), not a vestive remains. In 474 A.D. one Yayati
Keshari (a patriot), arose and expelled (or massacred) the
Yavanas. He founded the Singh dynasty which ruled till 1132
A.D. He built the Temple of Bhubaneswar. He says he found
Jagannath lying in the jungles and set him up again. This of
course means that he had another image made and re-established
the worship. He built a Temple on the site where the present
temple stands. Puri again became a city of Hindu pilgrimage,
and (we may say) assumed something of its present form. The
Singh Dynasty was succeeded by that of the Debs - a /5/
Bengali race. Ananga Bhima Deb (A.D.1175 to 1202) built the
Temple of Jagannath which now stands. The town of Puri seems
to have been little affected by the conquest of the Mughals, the
termination of the Rajas of Orissa in 1534 and their conversion
into Rajas of Khurda, the rebellion of the Orissa Afghans against
the Moghuls or the Mahratta conquest in 1756. The Mahrattas
levied a pilgrim tax on all persons coming on pilgrimage to
Puri.

In 1803 the British troops marched in from Narsinghpatna on
their way up from Ganjam. They appeared to the priests like a
second edition of Rakta Bahu, so they determined to make a
present of the temple to mollify the invaders. The arrival of the
troops was merely part of the general campaign against the
Mahrattas, and the general of course has orders from Lord
Wellesley to respect all rights and prejduces. The temple was
therefore left /6/ unharmed. The troops were in fact welcomed
as deliverers. The Rajas of Khurda became Rajas of Puri

SELECT BIBLIOGRAPHY

A Dictionary of Symbols — J.E. Girlot & J. Sage (London, 1962)

A History of Orissa, 2 vols. — WWW. Hunter, A. Stirling, J.Beams & N.K. Şahu (Calcutta,1956)

An Introduction to the Study of Ancient History — D.D. Kosambi

Ancient Geography of India, The — A. Cunningham

Ancient India — McCrindle (New Delhi reprint, 1973)

Ancient Indian Historical Tradition — F.E. Pargiter (Delhi reprint,1962)

Antiquities of Orissa, The, 2 vols. — Rajendra Lal Mitra (Calcuta reprint, 1963)

Archaeological Remains at Bhubaneswar — K.C. Panigrahi (Calcutta, 1961)

Bhilsa Topes — A. Cunningham (Varanasi reprint, 1966)

Bruton's Visit to Lord Jagannatha 350 years ago — (ed) P.T. Nair (Calcutta, 1985)

Buddhism in Tibet — Waddell (London, 1895)

Census of India

Chronology of the Bhauma-Karas and the Somavansis of Orissa—K.C. Panigrahi (Bhubaneswar, 1981)

Cult of Jagannath, The — K.C. Misra (Calcutta, 1971)

Cult of Jagannath and the Regional Traditions of Orissa, The — A. Eischman, H. Kulke and G.C. Tripathi (New Delhi, 1978)

Culture & Civilisation of Ancient India in Historical Outline — D.D. Kosambi (New Delhi, 1977)

Cultural Tradition in Puri — N.Patnaik (Simla, 1977)

Classical Accounts of India: The Greek and Roman Accounts of Ancient India — R C Majumdar (Calcutta, 1981)

Early Stone Temples of Orissa — V. Dehajia (New Delhi, 1979)

Encyclopaedia of Religion and Ethics, Vols.1-12

Epigraphica India, Vols. 11,13,15,23,28,30

Great Religions of the Modern World, The — Edward J.Jary (U.S.A.,1946)

Hindu Polytheism — Alain Danielou (London, 1913)

History of Indian and Eastern Architecture — J. Fergusson (London, 1910)

History and Culture of Orissa — (ed) M.N Das (Cuttack, 1977)

History of Jagannath Temple in the 19th Century — Prabhat Mukherjee (Calcutta, 1977)

History of Orissa, The, 2 vols. — Hare Krushna Mahtab (1959, 1960)

History of Orissa — K.C. Panigrahi (Cuttack, 1981)

History of Orissa, 2 vols. — R.D. Banerjee (Calcutta, 1930)

History of Pooree, The — B.K. Ghosh (Cuttack, 1848)

History of Oriya literature — Mayadhar Mansinha (New Delhi, 1962)

Jagannathuh Swami Nayanapathagami — Achyutananda (Calcutta. 1388 B.S.)

Legends of Jagannath Puri — R.K. Das (Bhadrak, 1981)

Life and Culture in Orissa — (ed) B.S. Das (Calcutta, 1984)

Literature and Social Life in Mediaeval Orissa — K.C. Sahoo (Bhubaneswar, 1981)

Migration of Symbols, The — G.d' Alvielle (U.S.A. 1894)

Orissa under Marathas, 1751-1803 — Bhabani Charan Ray (Allahabad, 1960)

Popular Religion and Folklore of North India — W. Crooke, (London, 1925)

Purana Text of the Dynasties of Kali Age, The — F.E. Pargiter (New Delhi reprint, 1975)

Religion of an Indian Tribe, The — Verrier Elwin (London: 1955)

Rising India — M. Jha (Delhi, 1978)

Saga of the Land of Lord Jagannath, The — Mayadhar Mansinha (Cuttack, n.d.)

Sambalpur Gazetter — L.S.S. O'Malley (Nagpur, 1919)

Things Indian — W. Crooke; (London,; 1906)

Totemism in India — J. K Ferreira (New Delhi, 1965)

Tribal India : A Synthetic View of Primitive Man (1978)

Tribal Myths of Eastern India — Edward T. Dalton (Calcutta, 1972)

Tribal Myths of Orissa — Verrier Elwin (London, 1954)

Tribal Religion — J. Troisi (New Delhi-1979)

Tribes and Castes of the Central Provinces of India— R. V. Russell and Hira Lal (London, 1969)

Typical Selections from Oriya Literature — B.C. Majumdar (Allahabad, 1921)

Twentieth Century Encyclopaedia of Religious Knowledge (U.S.A., 1885)

Vedic Mythology — A.A. Macdonald

Wanderings of a Pilgrim in Search of the Picturesque — F. Parkes (London, 1854)

B.
Vedas - Rk. and Atharva
Mahabharata
Harivamsha
Manusamhita
Katha Sarit Sagara
Banabhatta's *Kadambari* and *Harsacharita*
Markandeya Purana
Samba Purana
Skanda Purana
C.
Journal of Andhra Historical Research Society,
The Journal of Asiatic Society of Bengal
Orissa Historical Research Journal, The

INDEX